alia Khalil

Defining a Youth Leadership Pipeline for Egypt

Dearest Catoucha:

Hope you will enjoy my thoughts on youth leadership.

Dalia.

2016

Dalia Khalil

Defining a Youth Leadership Pipeline for Egypt

A realistic prospective on youth leadership development

LAP LAMBERT Academic Publishing

Impressum / Imprint
Bibliografische Information der Deutschen Nationalbibliothek: Die Deutsche Nationalbibliothek verzeichnet diese Publikation in der Deutschen Nationalbibliografie; detaillierte bibliografische Daten sind im Internet über http://dnb.d-nb.de abrufbar.
Alle in diesem Buch genannten Marken und Produktnamen unterliegen warenzeichen-, marken- oder patentrechtlichem Schutz bzw. sind Warenzeichen oder eingetragene Warenzeichen der jeweiligen Inhaber. Die Wiedergabe von Marken, Produktnamen, Gebrauchsnamen, Handelsnamen, Warenbezeichnungen u.s.w. in diesem Werk berechtigt auch ohne besondere Kennzeichnung nicht zu der Annahme, dass solche Namen im Sinne der Warenzeichen- und Markenschutzgesetzgebung als frei zu betrachten wären und daher von jedermann benutzt werden dürften.

Bibliographic information published by the Deutsche Nationalbibliothek: The Deutsche Nationalbibliothek lists this publication in the Deutsche Nationalbibliografie; detailed bibliographic data are available in the Internet at http://dnb.d-nb.de.
Any brand names and product names mentioned in this book are subject to trademark, brand or patent protection and are trademarks or registered trademarks of their respective holders. The use of brand names, product names, common names, trade names, product descriptions etc. even without a particular marking in this work is in no way to be construed to mean that such names may be regarded as unrestricted in respect of trademark and brand protection legislation and could thus be used by anyone.

Coverbild / Cover image: www.ingimage.com

Verlag / Publisher:
LAP LAMBERT Academic Publishing
ist ein Imprint der / is a trademark of
OmniScriptum GmbH & Co. KG
Heinrich-Böcking-Str. 6-8, 66121 Saarbrücken, Deutschland / Germany
Email: info@lap-publishing.com

Herstellung: siehe letzte Seite /
Printed at: see last page
ISBN: 978-3-659-75064-9

Zugl. / Approved by: University of Phoenix, Dissertation, 2012

Table of Contents

List of Tables

Chapter 1: Introduction

As a developing country, Egypt is facing a number of challenging obstacles, including an unemployment rate of 11.2% in 2005 and average inflation rate of 18.3% in 2008 (Economist Intelligence Unit, 2009). According to Save the Children (2010), 40% of Egyptian families suffer from poverty, 2.7 million children face child labor, and 95% of girls undergo female genital cutting. Young Egyptian new job seekers remain idle for an average of 7years (Save the Children, 2010). To overcome developmental needs, Egypt needs clear direction, resource allocation, and wise leadership (Galal, 2008). To aid Egypt in moving past these hurdles and establishing a pipeline for youth leadership development in Egypt, key issues such as youth and leadership should be addressed.

Chapter 1 includes the problem, purpose, and method of a qualitative study supported by quantitative data and modified Delphi research study to examine the competencies and behavior acquisition processes needed for young leaders. Chapter 1 also includes a discussion on the nature of the study, the significance of the study, and the conceptual framework that provides the foundation and justification for the study. The study involved examining the perceptions of a heterogeneous sample of local stakeholders consisting of educators, parents, youth, employers, and community leaders in the greater Cairo, Egypt, metropolitan area.

Background

According to the Center for Development and Population Activities (CEDPA, 2009), today's choices related to preparing youth for positive social, economic and political engagement, affect the future of the world. Leadership skills are becoming a necessary base for a successful life (Rogers & Wellins, 2010). The development of young people into confident, effective leaders helps to develop both youth and their communities (Pittman & Wright, 1991). Developing youth leadership skills increase problem-solving skills, self-esteem, and academic and career development as well as the ability to become actively involved in global societies (Brockman, Tepper, & MacNeil, 2007). From a broader development vision, researchers at the World Bank (2007) noted the lack of participation in and disengagement from community development can negatively affect youth development and welfare.

According to Helal, Ismail, and Gomaa (2000), Egypt is facing three major youth developmental problems: Egyptian students lack political participation, exhibit a shallow second leadership cadre, and face high rates of unemployment. Shehata (2008) noted how youth in Egypt is a disadvantaged group and suffering from different ways of social and economic exclusion. The exceedingly low levels of youth civic engagement in Egypt in the last six years are as follows: 56% of Egyptian youth had never voted in student union elections, 67% of Egyptian youth had never participated in any student activities, and 84% of Egyptian youth did not take part in any public protest or demonstration (Assaad & Barsoum, 2007). In the 2005 Egyptian presidential elections, young voters were the least represented segment of the voting population (British Broadcasting Corporation, 2005).

Rodman (2007) noticed an increasing recognition of the importance of integrating multidimensional youth leadership programs into educational systems. To become active local and global citizens, the leadership programs give youth the capacity to steer the complexities of an interconnected world (Rodman, 2007). Several international organizations and governments responded to the need for youth development and leadership. The agencies include the Association Internationale des Etudiants en Sciences Economiques et Commerciales (2006), Creative Youth Leadership Program (2009), and Rotary Youth Leadership Award (Rotary International, 2009).

According to the Economist Intelligence Unit (2009), citizens 10–14 years old represented 10.4% of the Egyptian population in 2008; citizens 15–19 years old accounted for 9.8% of the total population in 2008. Youth (ages 10–44) represented more than 58.9% of the population (Central Intelligence Agency [CIA], 2010; Egypt State Information Service, 2006b), with 21% aged 15 to 24 (Assaad & Roudi-Fahimi, 2007). Although young people are one of a country's main developmental tools, Egyptian youth do not gain adequate leadership skills during their schooling years, college years, or as adults (American Chamber of Commerce, 2008). Egyptian public universities lack offerings in leadership development services and activities (International Youth Foundation, 2007).

At the secondary schooling level, youth activities are not tailored toward civic engagement, service learning, and leadership development (CEDPA, 2009). A few isolated experiences are available through extracurricular programs and funded projects in a limited number of schools. According to CEDPA (2009), young Egyptians, who constitute 70 percent of Egypt's population, face high unemployment and poverty. Traditional institutions that are expected to assist youth in developing strategies to overcome national challenges lack the necessary means and structure. The World Bank (2007) concluded, "As the focus of activities on youth is still new there is yet not much information on the work that is done on youth and respectively the needs youth face these days" (p. 5), and youth contributions toward societal development are untapped.

Human rights advocates commented negatively on the repression of the youth during the political change movement (Azarva, 2006). Society and parents learn from governmental actions and do not encourage their children and youth to participate in school or nonschool leadership development to avoid future problems or arrests (Serageldin, 2006). In reference to the latest economic revival since 2004, Egyptian youth have been the most misfortunate group in terms of unemployment, salaries, restricted job security and steadiness, education credentials, and limited channels for exercising citizenship (Assaad & Barsoum, 2007).

Jennings, Parra-Medina, Messias, and McLoughlin (2006) identified a need for practice-based research to identify how the engagement of youth in critical youth empowerment programs can influence youth in different ways. Few research studies and initiatives have included a focus on the deficiency of knowledge and technical skills of schools and college graduating students (American Chamber of Commerce, 2008; Assaad & Barsoum, 2007; British Council, 2005; Egyptian International Economic Forum, 2009). As the majority of the initiatives with a focus on youth in Egypt were funded projects, sustainability has become a challenge (Kasim & Shah, 2008). The current research study addresses part of that challenge.

Problem Statement

For sustainable economies in developing nations such as Egypt, well-qualified youth should take on leadership roles in their communities (Zedan, 2007). For the benefit of society worldwide, nations and educational organizations should encourage and develop diversified youth leadership programs through the advancement of understanding and practice (J. R. Alexander, 2006). Youth are tomorrow's leaders, and youth leadership is a priority (Youth Leadership Initiative, 2007).

The general problem addressed in the current study was the lack of adequate opportunities for young adults to develop and practice leadership in Egypt (United Nations Volunteers, 2008). On both formal and informal levels, students and young adults are not encouraged to voice their opinions, practice citizenship, and participate in leadership training and education (Helal et al., 2000). Due to social, economic, and political barriers, Egyptian youth face obstacles to empowerment and a state of marginalization (Al-Ghanim, 2005). The specific problem was the absence of information and understanding about the needed youth leadership competencies, processes, and evaluative tools to build effective leadership programs (Shokr, 2004). A study was necessary to fill the gap in the knowledge base.

Purpose

The qualitative study supported by quantitative data with a modified Delphi design involved exploring and identifying the needed leadership competencies, processes, and evaluative tools for the development of Egyptian youth leadership programs in the future targeting young adults between the ages of 15 and 24. The purpose of the study was to explore, examine, and refine the leadership skills and competencies needed for young leaders in Egypt; to determine how to develop multiple youth development and leadership opportunities for youth at ages 15–24; and to establish necessary effective evaluative methods. The unit for study was the leadership competencies that need incorporating into successful youth leadership programs.

In the study, 40 identified experts participated in a three-round survey to gain consensus on the competencies needed to develop appropriate and effective youth leadership programs for youth between the ages of 15 and 24. As available literature lacked the knowledge and consensus about youth leadership competencies, processes, and evaluative methods, a modified Delphi design was expected to be the best fit to ensure the fulfillment of the goals and objectives for the current research. Identified experts included educators, parents, youth, employers, and community leaders.

The Delphi method is future oriented (Rice, 2009) and helps to ensure the provision of adequate answers to research questions. The Delphi design can assist in specific real-world issues such as planning programs, assessing needs, determining policies, using resources, developing alternatives, exploring assumptions, and correlating collective judgment (Hsu & Sanford, 2007a). The current study involved identifying leadership competencies for youth ages 15–24 for the development and evaluation of programs in the future. The geographical location of the study was the greater Cairo zone, which includes Cairo, Giza, Helwan, Sixth of October, and El Qualubia governorates. All identified stakeholders were from urban locations to ensure their personal and professional exposure to leadership opportunities as participants and observers.

Significance of the Study

The study was the first of its nature in Egypt to focus on defining leadership competencies for young adults (age 15–24) in the 21st century. The focus of earlier studies was on problematic issues related to youth, such as drug prevention, child labor, and juvenile delinquency (Egypt State Information Service, 2006a). Ibrahim et al. (1999) conducted a national survey from a reproductive health perspective in 1997 that included 9,000 adolescents (10–19 years old) and their parents. The focus of the study was on examining the social relationships adolescents have toward family and peers, the transition to marriage, reproductive roles, and characteristics of adolescent marriage especially for females. The International Institute of Social Studies (2009) conducted a qualitative, comparative study using case study research methods in seven countries, including Egypt, with a focus on "rights, gender equity, lifestyle changes, and virtual media, in a more in-depth exploration of questions of violence, insecurity, and vulnerability (and their antitheses: peace and security) in the lives of children and youth" (para. 3). The study was designed to benefit different segments of society including educators, social researchers, policy makers, parents, nongovernmental agencies, and funding agencies for the development of leadership programs for youth ages 15–24 in the future.

Significance of Study to Leadership

The results of the study may help youth leaders and educators to design, establish, and assess youth leadership programs through formal or informal educational activities. The study adds to studies on leadership and youth development and may serve as a model for additional studies. The study provides a foundation of information that can contribute to a change in perception and application of Egyptian youth empowerment and leadership from one of rehabilitation and prevention to one of development and educational priority.

Leaders who conduct research studies may benefit from examining the process of decision and policy making (Creswell, 2005). The current research was intended to extend the study of youth leadership to new geographical regions, topics, and research areas; voice the underserved or less represented samples in the community; and benefit leaders, practitioners, and policy makers. Results of the study contribute to new understandings and practices in youth empowerment and leadership in developing countries. The study included practical models of youth leadership programs for cultural validation, implementation, and evaluation in other countries in the Middle East and North Africa (MENA) region.

Nature of the Study

The qualitative study supported by quantitative data with modified Delphi design involved exploring and identifying the needed leadership competencies, processes, and evaluative tools for the development of Egyptian youth leadership programs targeting young adults between the ages of 15 and 24. The results are expected to be used to develop multiple youth development and leadership opportunities for youth aged 15–24 years old and to establish necessary effective evaluative methods. A major goal of the modified Delphi study was to determine the leadership competencies needed by Egyptian youth. The study included educators, parents, youth (19–24), employers, and community leaders.

Qualitative and quantitative research studies differ in the types of problems considered, handling of literature, research purpose and questions, use and analysis of data, and writing and structure of the research report (Neuman, 2003). Quantitative research is an unbiased and objective study done through asking specific and narrow questions, collecting numbers and data, and conducting analysis (Creswell, 2005). The researcher sets the questions and hypotheses. A qualitative study includes asking broad and general questions to explore the views of the research participants, collecting data that rely on words and text, and analyzing data in a more subjective manner (de Vaus, 2006).

The Delphi begins with a qualitative approach where open-ended seed questions are a vehicle to determine theories and constructs that can be used in the future (Zhao, 2007). Subsequent rounds of questioning are quantitative in nature as the concepts that emerge in Round 1 are tested and consensus is sought. Youth empowerment and leadership is a social action process with multiple levels such as "individual, family, organization, and community" (Jennings et al., 2006, p. 33). The sample involved a Delphi panel including stakeholders from each interval of the life spectrum of a young leader. Different researchers have used the Delphi method with multiple stakeholders (Greenhalgh & Wengraf, 2008; Keil, Tiwana, & Bush, 2002; Macdonald, 2003; Malcolm, Knighting, Forbat, & Kearney, 2009; Manca, Varnhagen, Brett-Maclean, Allan, & Szafran, 2008; J. Martin, 1991; Masberg, Chase, & Madlem, 2003; Owens, Ley, & Aiten, 2008; Rice, 2009; Stolper et al., 2009; Toth, 1996). The purposively selected stakeholders included educators, parents of young leaders, youth (19–24 years old), employers, and community leaders.

First, young leaders are influenced by parental choices, values, child-rearing style, involvement, and socioeconomic level. Parents were included to describe the methods and techniques they used with their young leaders at home and to elaborate on the overall support system they used to foster young leaders. Marsh and Willis (2003) identified parental involvement in school decision making as the seventh and most active level of involvement. Second, educators from different levels of education, such as teachers and college professors, affect young leaders. Third, young leaders are affected by their own innate character and motivational levels. In the study, young leaders were included to provide input regarding ways individual experiences have assisted in and contributed to their own leadership development.

Fourth, employers shape market needs and associated skills to assist young leaders to fit into a competitive medium for employment (British Council, 2005; American Chamber of Commerce, 2008). Fifth, feedback from community leaders was important to reflect the societal values, cultural customs and traditions, and future leadership needs of communities. Society has the right to voice its future needs and expected outcomes from the educational process (Galal, 2008). Community involvement and continuous assessment are essential elements for educational reform and will enhance civil participation and public accountability (Middle East Institute, 2008).

Experts or stakeholders are selected for Delphi method studies based on background knowledge, previous experience, willing to contribute to the study, availability, and ability to communicate effectively (Skulmoski, Hartman, & Krahn, 2007). In the research study, the sample was chosen according to objective and expert-level criteria. The research participants who were parents would have volunteered to serve on leadership-level positions related to the age group 15–24 (e.g., school boards and sports clubs), reared children or youth (15–24 years old), and encouraged their children or youth to join activities with a leadership focus (e.g., Scouts), whether in Egypt or abroad. One parent per family was welcomed to have a diversity of families represented in the study.

Participants who were educators were chosen based on the level of participation (voluntarily or task-based) in the development and implementation of youth leadership activities (e.g., student councils). The sample included educators serving youth (15–24 years old). The sample of educators included teachers, professors, principals, and counselors.

The youth members included emerging adults (ages 19–24). The youth panel members needed to have participated in a leadership role during their high school years or college life in Egypt or abroad (e.g., president of an activity club). This group included students at public or private educational institutes.

The employer stakeholders included representatives from different sectors of employers: nongovernmental organizations, the private sector, the public sector, multinational organizations, and small and medium enterprises. The employer category participants needed to be either the owner or the chief executive of an organization known to be adopting policies and cultural environments encouraging empowerment and leadership among its entry-level positions (Egyptian International Economic Forum, 2009).

The community leader members were graduates of the Youth Socialism Institute in Egypt in the 1960s. Community leaders needed to hold a voluntarily leadership position (e.g., board member) in a community-based organization promoting the development and implementation of activities with a focus on youth development and leadership for ages 15–24. Community leaders included religious, political, social, and entrepreneurial representatives.

Data confidentiality was ensured because only the researcher was aware of the participants' identities. Researchers should consider a number of ethical standards: avoiding harm, delegation to and supervision of subordinates, documentation of professional and scientific work, and fees and financial agreements (American Psychological Association, 2002). Ethical standards also include avoidance of false or deceptive statements, limits of confidentiality, confidentiality of information and records, ownership of records and data, planning research, responsibility, institutional approval, informed consent to research, reporting of results, plagiarism, and publication credit. The study included efforts to be gender sensitive (Flick, 2009). To ensure the inclusion of the female perspective, gender equality, and participation diversity, the study sample targeted more than 50% female participation (Babbie, 2007).

The study included questionnaires as the main instrument for data collection over three rounds of circulation among the Delphi stakeholders. A pilot study was conducted to test the questionnaire questions for the first round of the Delphi tiers. Data analysis occurred continuously throughout the succeeding three rounds of the Delphi method. At the end of each round, the results from the different stakeholders were summarized, listed, and included in the following round of the questionnaire process (Bucknall, 2001). The collected data among the five stakeholder groups were coded and decoded. Through data analysis, the researcher tried to find agreements among each stakeholder and across the five stakeholder groups using qualitative analysis (Skulmoski et al., 2007). When using many Delphi stakeholders, Duffield (1993) suggested setting a baseline mean for item inclusion before starting the Delphi rounds and comparing panel results. The demographics of the population were also taken into consideration in the analysis process.

Research Questions

Research questions transform the purpose statement to precise questions to be answered by the researcher (Creswell, 2005). Qualitative studies include the use of research questions rather than hypotheses (Flick, 2009). The research questions are used to design the study, including the data collection procedures about a single concept or a central phenomenon, encouraging participants' ideas, and building general themes from those ideas (Neuman, 2003). In this qualitative study supported by quantitative data, the research questions were used to establish a consensus regarding needed competencies for effective youth leadership development programs. The qualitative approach is inductive and open to changes during the research process (de Vaus, 2006). In the study, the research questions were open-ended general questions with a central question (RQ1) and sub questions (RQ2 and RQ3).

The research questions played the role of a roadmap for the study. The study included three research questions:

RQ1: What are the needed competencies for youth development and leadership for Egyptian citizens between the ages of 15 and 24?

RQ2: What are the needed processes to build and deliver youth development and leadership programs for Egyptian citizens between the ages of 15 and 24?

RQ3: What are the needed evaluative tools to ensure effective implementation of youth development and leadership programs for Egyptian citizens between the ages of 15 and 24?

The research questions gave a comprehensive solution for the identified problem. The research questions were expected to result in answers about the competencies, processes, and evaluative methods needed to develop youth development and leadership programs in Egypt in the future for youth between the ages of 15 and 24. The three research questions were answered through a series of modified Delphi questionnaires and through reaching consensus among the stakeholders. Starting in Round 2, participants were requested to prioritize their summarized and agreed upon responses through a 5-point Likert-type scale (Macdonald, 2003).

Theoretical Framework

Biological, cognitive, psychological, and social changes affect adolescents (Lerner, Noh, & Wilson, 1998). Researchers and educators need to consider all factors, surroundings, and relations affecting adolescents. The development contextualization theory explains individual-context relations through the occurring social system or subsystems (Lerner et al., 1998). The development contextualization is an ecological perspective of human development (Lerner et al., 2005). Effective youth empowerment needs an encouraging and safe environment, active engagement to affect change, equality in power sharing with adults, welcoming of critical reflection, and integrated citizen and society-level empowerment (Jennings et al., 2006). Ecological development helps to realize the complexity and dynamic processes in the environment (Fraser, 1996). The research study included the use of developmental contextualization or ecological development. The adoption of developmental contextualization helped to explore the views of the youth environment stakeholders in Egypt and answer the identified research questions to reach a group consensus.

Based on the theory of developmental contextualization, Lerner et al. (2005) focused on the concept of youth as a resource, rather than threat, for development through mutual influential relationships. Youth interact with their "biological, psychological, ecological (family, community, culture), and historical niche" (p. 20). Lerner et al. referred to the emergence of the new term *positive youth development*. The foundation of positive youth development was the five Cs approaches consisting of competence, confidence, connection, character, and caring. The research study used developmental contextualization within the context of Egyptian youth and its surrounding environment and stakeholders, who are educators, parents, older youth, employers, and community leaders.

The research study is based on the youth development theory, which is inspired by three basic theories of child development and learning: Dewey's experiential learning, Vygotsky's zone of proximal development, and Bandura's social learning theory. Experiential learning theory (Dewy, 1938) is based on constructivism belief that the cognitive processes happen at both the physical and the social context, enforcing a strong relationship between learners and situations. The research study included Dewey's experiential learning in considering youth as a stakeholder in the selected sample. The sample included youth leaders (19-24 years).

Vygotsky's sociocultural theory (Theory into Practice, 2009) suggests youth leadership is a result of the integration of a number of factors and stakeholders influencing the development of young leaders. The research included the sociocultural theory in the selection of sample participants who represented the youth environment. The sample included educators, parents, youth (19–24 years), employers, and community leaders.

Learning Theories Knowledge base (2009) referred to Bandura's social learning theory, which bridges the transition from behaviorism to cognition in certain environmental factors, and posited that humans have the ability to observe, imitate, and learn from each other. The focus of social learning theory or the modeling process is on attention, memory, and motivation. For effective modeling, essential conditions such as attention, retention, reproduction, and motivation must be present. The study identified educators, parents, older youth, employers, and community leaders as the direct stakeholders who stimulate the modeling process in youth learning and development.

Definitions

Definitions selected for the study were from fields of professional development and education. The terms defined included competencies, leadership competencies, youth, and youth leadership development. Definitions assisted in offering context and meaning for the terms used.

Competencies: Clark (2008) related competencies to abilities due to expertise and experience. A competency is the qualification that asserts performance of a task (Wiggins, 1999).

Leadership competencies: Leaders are usually characterized with specific leadership traits such as "intelligence, dominance, sociability, self-monitoring, high energy and drive, self-confidence, and a tolerance for ambiguity" (Boseman, 2008, p. 36). For future leaders in a professional context, Beinecke and Spencer (2007) identified needed leadership competencies as personal skills and knowledge, interpersonal skills, transactional skills, transformational skills, policy, and program knowledge.

Youth: Youth includes individuals between the ages of 15 and 24, representing 18% of the world's population, with 85% in developing countries (United Nations, 2004). For the purpose of this research, youth were individuals ranging in age from 15 to 24.

Youth leadership development: Ricketts and Rudd (2002) noted youth leadership development studies are limited because most leadership studies were mainly focused on managerial and adult leadership. In the research study, youth leadership development referred to the process of developing young leaders through formal or informal settings to match priorities outlined in the national developmental plan.

Assumptions

In a scholarly study, participants are expected to be honest and participatory toward the data collection method and requests for input (Neuman, 2003). The participants were assumed to believe in the existence of the problem, had a personal and professional interest in the outcome of the study, and would be willing to contribute to the development process of future programs in youth leadership (Maxwell, 2006). Study participants were expected to contribute actively to the three rounds of the Delphi study. Participants were also expected to participate in the controlled feedback following each round of questionnaires. Because the study was administered in English, participants were expected to be proficient in reading and writing English to comprehend the questionnaire instrument used for the data collection. The Delphi stakeholders were expected to have some university-level education. The questionnaires were expected to elicit the information needed to respond to the research questions. The study was expected to present a solid base of knowledge for starting the development of youth leadership programs in Egypt and to encourage future research and development in this neglected area.

Scope, Limitations, and Delimitations

The study included a number of research limitations and boundaries. The focus of the research was on leadership competencies of youth between the ages of 15 and 24 in the metropolitan area of Cairo, Egypt. The stakeholders in youth leadership included educators, parents, youth (19–24 years old), employers, and community leaders.

Limitations

A major limiting factor was the busy schedules of the selected experts. The study worked around the experts' schedules and several reminders were sent to the experts to ensure they would respond in a timely manner. The study's data collection was simple and focused to reduce the time experts spend responding to the questionnaires. Starting in the second Delphi round, participants received a summary of their earlier responses.

Under a scientifically based research framework, Denzin, Lincoln, and Giardina (2006) noted qualitative research is suspected of not having well-defined variables or causal models and is subjective. Designs of qualitative studies do not generate systematic generalization to broad population (Maxwell, 2002). Myers (2000) noted research paradigms are affected by "philosophical, theoretical, instrumental, and methodological foundations" (p. 1). The research results were determined by the participants' viewpoints and might not be generalized due to the small size of the sample researched. Therefore, generalization was affected.

Another limitation was the number of resources on youth leadership references, statistics, and programs in Egypt. Most resources about Egypt's statistics were from international agencies rather than national organizations. Another challenge was the researcher's independent status, which prevented her from receiving appropriate access to national data. To overcome researcher bias, an objective position was maintained by expressing tested views in recent years about youth leadership development and portraying the views in the Egyptian setting. The study did not involve testing the appropriateness of literature collected mostly by researchers from the United States and the Western hemisphere with regard to its adjustability and fitness to the Egyptian culture, values, and context.

Delimitation

The first delimitation consisted of a target sample size of 40 invited experts representing five different identified stakeholder groups, which included educators, parents, youth, employers, and community leaders. Although the five categories represented the major stakeholders involved in youth leadership, the categories and sample size did not represent all stakeholders influencing youth leadership development and implementation. The results might not be generalizable due to the small sample size compared to the overall population of Egypt and specifically the greater Cairo area, where the research took place. The use of heterogeneous groups can complicate the process of data collection and analysis, achieving consensus, and verifying results (Zami & Lee, 2009). Limiting the research to greater Cairo and urban locations did not give any opportunity for interested experts from other locations outside greater Cairo who might have insightful feedback to participate in the study. Because of this delimitation, the study was not able to represent the rural population in Egypt, which represents 67% of the total population (CIA, 2009), and its culture, needs, and progress.

After comparing Polish and Dutch leadership, Koenig (2008) discovered that culture influences leadership. Because of the same delimitations, the study could not also be generalizable to other regions (e.g., MENA). Further studies might be necessary to explore the possibility of implementing the study results in different geographical areas. Time, money, and resources limited the application of results to Egypt and did not allow for a global solution.

The data collection method involved the modified Delphi method operated through Web-based questionnaires. According to Internet World Stats (2009), 12.9% of Egyptians use the Internet. The delivery method might have been limiting to some stakeholders who were not competent in technology and use of e-mail. As the limitation might have affected the level of participation and the response rate of experts, participants were able to express their preference in responding to questionnaires through Web-based or hard-copy questionnaires. Necessary formatting would have been applied to both formats to ensure reliability of the data collection instrument.

Summary

Chapter 1 included a discussion on the general problem, which was the lack of adequate opportunities for young adults to develop and practice leadership in Egypt (Middle East Youth Initiative, 2008; United Nations Development Programme [UNDP], 2007). On both formal and informal levels, Egyptian young adults are not encouraged to voice their opinions, practice citizenship, and participate in leadership training and education. The specific problem was the deficiency in identifying the needed youth leadership competencies, processes, and evaluative tools to build effective leadership programs.

Chapter 1 included background about the selected problem, problem statement, purpose, significance of the study, nature of the study, research questions, theoretical framework, definitions, assumptions, scope, limitations, and delimitations. The study included three research questions: RQ1 concerning needed competencies for youth development and leadership, RQ2 concerning needed processes to develop youth development and leadership programs, and RQ3 concerning needed evaluative tools to ensure the effective implementation of youth development and leadership for Egyptian citizens between the ages of 15 and 24.

Through a modified Delphi technique with three rounds of questionnaires, the study was expected to answer the research questions and provide creative solutions to the identified problem. The participants were 40 experts in the fields of adolescence and youth leadership representing educators, parents, youth (19–24 years), employers, and community leaders. The definition section included definitions about competencies, leadership competencies, youth, and youth leadership development. Chapter 1 also included an introduction to the adopted theoretical framework, which is the development contextualization and positive youth development concept (Lerner et al., 2005). The theoretical framework also included Dewey's experiential learning, Vygotsky's zone of proximal development, and Bandura's social learning theory.

Chapter 2 will include the literature review with a detailed exploration of youth leadership development in Egypt in the 1960s (Shokr, 2004) and other countries in the first decade of the 21 century. Chapter 2 will have sections on germinal theories, a historical overview, gaps of knowledge, and current theories. The chapter will also include literature on best practices in other countries.

Chapter 2: Review of the Literature

The research study involved exploring needed leadership competencies for young adults (15–24 years old) in Egypt. The study involved an exploration into the effective processes and evaluative methods and tools needed for programs promoting leadership for young adults. Chapter 2 contains an overview of earlier research in the field of youth empowerment, leadership, and development through a literature review. The literature review is "a written summary of journal articles, books, and other documents that describes the past and current state of information, organizes the literature into topics and documents a need for a proposal study" (Creswell, 2005, p. 79). In a qualitative study, the literature review needs to come at the beginning of the study to justify the importance of the research problem. Through the literature review, researchers become aware of the knowledge gaps in the researched area (Cone & Foster, 1993).

The research study involved identifying key terms, locating literature, critically evaluating and selecting literature, organizing the literature, and writing a review (Creswell, 2005; Neuman, 2003). Chapter 2 contains a comprehensive review of literature related to terms such as youth, youth empowerment, youth leadership, youth development, leadership competencies, processes involved in youth development programs, and evaluative methods. For a developmental plan, the study involved exploring earlier practices in youth leadership programs and initiatives in Egypt and other countries. The selection of countries included both developed and developing countries. The chapter also includes a conclusion and a summary section.

Documentation

Ruszkiewicz, Walker, and Pemberton (2006) suggested diversifying the types of literature as summaries, encyclopedias, dictionaries and glossaries of terms, handbooks, statistical indexes, reviews and syntheses, books, journals, abstract series, indexes, and databases. The current research includes a variety of resources related to youth in Egypt, the Middle East region, and the world. The resources were sought mainly through a virtual environment due to the lack of access to and existence of specialized libraries in Egypt. The resources were obtained from the University of Phoenix library and other recognizable and valid online websites. A number of search engines as Google and Yahoo were employed. Sage, ProQuest and ProQuest Dissertations and Theses, Gale Power Search, Academic Exchange, and EBSCOhost were also used. A valuable book that includes an evaluative study about the Youth Socialism Institute in Egypt during the period of 1963-1976 was located (Shokr, 2004). Personal and professional networks also proved helpful in finding more resources and experts in the fields of youth development and leadership. The primary documents spanned the years 2005–2011. Certain documents were outside the scope of this period but were appropriate and significant to the historical background of the issues researched. Depicted in Table 1 is the reference matrix.

In the research study, the resources were selected based upon the date of publication (mostly in the duration 2005–2010), peer reviewed, and with a focus on youth development and leadership. Key words used for searching were *youth, youth empowerment, youth leadership, extracurricular activities, leadership competencies, adolescences, youth development opportunities,* and *Egypt.* The resources were first reviewed through a skimming and scanning process with a focus on relevance to the study. All resources were classified and saved on the computer according to their database and date retrieved. Then resources were printed for easier reading. In each resource, key items such as references, abstract, research design and type, methods, discussion, and results were highlighted. Older references referred to leadership theories under Egypt's former political status; many were listed as secondary resources. Primary sources were preferred over secondary resources in the study. Although new sources are considered more suitable for a research study, the socioeconomic and political environment of Egypt negatively affected the availability of sources on the topic of leadership, especially youth leadership. A high percentage of the older references were published between 2002 and 2004, reflecting a change in the political environment of Egypt, possibly the result of the influence of Gamal Mubarak, President Mubarak's son, who is associated with a neoliberal movement (Trofimov, 2009).

Table 1

Reference Matrix

Source implemented	*n*
Government directives	5
Peer-reviewed articles	114
Reports	25
Conference papers	5
Books	93
Periodicals	6
Guides	3
Doctoral dissertations	15
Websites	56

    Creswell (2005) characterized scholarly work that cites original sources as appropriate for research study. Original sources give truth and reliance, share the originality of the work, and give credit to the creator of this knowledge (Denzin & Lincoln, 2000). Locating original sources is also part of the ethical code of research (American Psychological Association, 2010). Finding original sources before including them in the literature review is one of the steps of preparation before starting the writing process (Neuman, 2003). The research steps include identifying key terms to use for searching, locating literature in library resources, evaluating the materials, and relating the source with the study; managing and preparing the materials of the literature review; and writing the literature review (McMillan & Schumacher, 2006). In the literature review, the suggested research steps were followed.

    A theoretical or conceptual framework is used to generate a theory or explore a concept (Creswell, 2005; Maner, 2000). In a qualitative study, a conceptual framework is evident throughout the research with a theoretical highlight at the end of the study (Neuman, 2003). The results might confirm or disagree with current and available theories (Maxwell, 2006). In the research study, relevant theoretical frames were identified, adapted, and adjusted for use within the Egyptian context (Miller & Salkind, 2002).

Germinal Theories

Human development theories form the basis for the current understanding about learning, leadership, and development (Wittrock, 2010). The main human development theories need to be studied to explore links with current understanding and development in the area of leadership. This section included a discussion on the change in human development theories from behaviorism to social learning through constructivism and experiential learning and the relationship between the change in human development theories and the Egyptian context, as appropriate. This section ended with a focus on the underlying theory of the research study, which was developmental contextualization (Lerner et al., 2005).

Historical overview. Schunk (2004) highlighted the major difference between the main poles of the human development theories, which are behaviorism and cognition, and commented on the importance of both theory and practice to develop and refine one another. Chung (2005) tried to settle the contradiction among theorists and practitioners in the field of education development. Whitmore (2004) differentiated between the behavioral approach, which considers the relationship between observable behaviors and patterns of external stimuli, and the cognitive approach, which considers the relationship between information flow, the mind, conceptualization, and information-processing system.

Although human development theories have been through many paradigms, Egypt's educational system is at the early stages of the behaviorist era, which Schunk (2004) described as "explain[ing] learning in terms of environment events" (p. 29). Among the different behaviorists, Guthrie's approach was relevant to Egypt's case. According to Schunk, Guthrie believed that human behaviors based on observable measures, contiguity of stimuli and responses, associated strength, reward and punishment, and habit formation. According to Stevens, Wineburg, Herrenkohl, and Bell (2005), behaviorists did not care enough for domain specificity. The behavior focus was on the issues of shaping, reinforcement, and contingency, which did not help in deeply explaining how to learn.

Behavioral theorists view learning as an observable phenomenon with the formation of stimuli or response associations (Whitmore, 2004). Memory consists of neurological connections to external stimuli, whereas motivation consists of the increased rate of behavioral occurrence resulting from reinforcement (Stevens et al., 2005). Instruction should be based on the understanding of formed stimuli–response associations and selective reinforcement (Schunk, 2004).

Jonassen (2006) noted that constructivism, which considers learning to be an active and constructive process (Learning Theories Knowledgebase, 2009), is not a theory of learning or a model for designing instruction but an epistemology. Constructivism supports the ability of instructional innovations to support meaningful learning (e.g., anchored instruction, problem-based learning, cognitive tools, and simulations). Schunk (2004) explained learners are responsible for constructing their own understanding of knowledge rather than being imposed upon from outside or happening automatically. As a core premise, constructivists believe the cognitive processes happen at both the physical and the social context, enforcing a strong relationship between learners and situations (Dewey, 1938). Vygotsky's (Theory into Practice, 2009) contribution to constructivism was through his sociocultural theory, which considered the social environment as the catalyst for development and learning, including culture, language, symbols, and social associations.

The research study included Vygotsky's sociocultural theory adopted through an assumption that youth leadership is a result of the integration of a number of factors and stakeholders influencing the development of young leaders. The research also included the sociocultural theory in the selection of sample participants who represented the youth environment. The sample included educators, parents, youth (19–24 years), employers, and community leaders.

Schunk (2004) supported Piaget's conclusion that learning happens as children experience the world's concepts from their own perspectives and proceed with information from surrounding environments. Children and young learners reach additional complex views through increasing experiences. For youth, Rose (2006) identified external and internal factors for learning. The external factors include empowerment, expectations, and effective use of time. The internal factors include motivation, commitment, positive values and identity, and interpersonal skills. Dewey (1938) noted that experiences help learners form "attitudes of desire and purpose" (p. 39). The research study included Piaget's and Dewey's conclusions about progressiveness and experiential learning in considering youth as a stakeholder in the selected sample. Youth insights, voices, and experiences were considered in the study.

Learning Theories Knowledge base (2009) referred to Bandura's social learning theory, which bridges the transition from behaviorism to cognition in certain environmental factors, and posited that humans have the ability to observe, imitate, and learn from each other. The focus of social learning theory or the modeling process is on attention, memory, and motivation. For effective modeling, essential conditions such as attention, retention, reproduction, and motivation must be present. Libby, Sedonaen, and Bliss (2006) suggested people involved in the youth leadership development process should consider and build on positive youth–adult partnerships. The study also included the social learning theory in assuming the vital role of direct youth environments on the formation and development of youth leadership. The study identified educators, parents, older youth, employers, and community leaders as the direct stakeholders who stimulate the modeling process in youth learning and development.

Jonassen (2006) noted that neither a best model of instruction nor a theory of learning exists, as no existing model or theory can predict a learner's acquisition of knowledge; educators and decision makers need to be epistemologically mature. Chung (2005) suggested that education development is complex and warned educators against adopting theoretical resources without considering youth needs. Youth programs need to focus on youth developmental needs and consider the youths' muscle, cognition, and emotion. Youth leadership can be a possible outcome from youth development. Youth programs should have a greater focus on the youth developmental process rather than on one outcome or component. Youth development theory is based on three basic theories of child development and learning: Dewey's experiential learning, Vygotsky's zone of proximal development, and Bandura's social learning theory.

Lerner et al. (2005) called for the consideration of developmental contextualization, which refers to an appreciation of the ecological factor in human development. According to Gruber and Mandl (2001), constructivist learning environments are based on the assumptions that individuals are mentally constructive and learning is embedded in a social manner and accelerating participation in specialized communities of practice. Rich and authentic learning environments contribute positively to the development of gifted and talented children and youth. Pelletier and Corter (2006) examined the interplay between intersecting elements of school, culture, governmental policies, public and private sectors, parents, family, and neighborhood. By adopting social ecology, children and youth will be looked at from a holistic point of view and as a product of an integrated system. Social ecology is the consideration of links and interactions within a child and youth context (e.g., parents, educators, peers) through nested levels of influence over an ontogenetic change within youth and culture. Social ecology or developmental contextualization theory for human development promotes integration (Lerner et al., 2005). The developmental contextualization concept comprised the theoretical framework for the current study.

Current theories. This section includes an exploration of current leadership theories. Beinecke and Spencer (2007) noted that current leadership theories are characterized as systematic in sharing information and values, effective communication, and empowered and responsible members. Beinecke and Spencer believed in a flexible leadership model able to adapt to serve the needs and interests of stakeholders' networks. Among the main recommendations of the World Bank (2007), researchers suggested considering youth as a community asset and noted the need for conducting specialized research studies with a focus on youth development and issues. Research results need to be shared and publicized for all youth-led and youth organizations interested in youth development in Egypt. The study contributes to the research area of youth leadership and assists in developing effective leadership programs for youth ages 15–24 in Egypt.

A theoretical framework should be the basis of youth development leadership. According to Harrison (1999), a series of developments in leadership understanding occurred during the 20th century. Between 1900 and 1930, the focus of leadership was the control and centralization of power. During the 1930s, the focus of leadership was on trait and group processes. During the 1940s and 1950s, literature was dominated by the group approach theory and leadership as a relationship that develops shared goals. During the 1960s, the focus of leadership was as a behavior that influences people. During the 1970s, the organizational behavior approach of management emerged. During the 1980s, a theory of excellence, which was considered a descendant of the greatman theory, spread among scholars and professionals.

Since 1980, new theories of leadership emerged featuring charismatic, visionary, and transformational leadership. By the end of the 20th century, a number of other models were developed. According to Bolman and Deal (2003), leadership has moved through different stages and styles. Leadership can be structural, human resource-oriented, political, or symbolic. Bolman and Deal added, leaders are aware of their own strengths, can develop them, and form teams that can perform leadership under the four models of leadership. Human resource leadership was widely used in the 1960s and 1970s (Harrison, 1999). The leadership trend moved into symbolic and visionary leadership to perform cultural transformation. MacNeil (2006) explained how leadership studies evolved and developed over the years, moving from the great man theory to the trait theory, then to group and organizational focus, to behavioral and motivational theories, and finally to management sciences. The new trends focus more on cooperative leadership than on the earlier concepts of the one-man-show approach. Functional frames of leadership consider leadership processes rather than leaders' characteristics (MacNeil, 2006). The following section includes an explanation of different leadership styles.

Trait theory. Wren (2004) described the trait theory as a theory in which leaders have technical skills, and personal qualities. Sheard and Kakabadse (2004) noted that leadership should not be considered only on personal characteristics; leadership must be valued from the perspective of individual role and team involvement. Cawthon (1992) reported researchers and organizational leaders should examine leadership using a more expanded horizon and not limit it to a mere study of traits, behaviors, or contingencies. Shriberg, Barnhart, and Shriberg (2002) referred to the way modern theories of leadership have been affected by Gardner's identified leadership traits such as physical vivacity and stamina, intelligence and practical judgment, sense of responsibility, task-based competence, understanding followers' needs, managing people, seeking achievement, ability to motivate people, courage, credibility, decisiveness, self-assurance, assertiveness, and flexibility. Shriberg et al. classified the personal characteristics as physical, personality, social, intelligence, and work-related traits. In the Egyptian context, President Nasser is a clear example of a trait leader due to his charisma and personal characteristics (Chary, 2004).

Transactional leadership. Transactional leadership is also called directive and autocratic leadership. The transactional model relies on coercive power and includes direction, power, identified goals, pressure, and the use of threatening mechanisms to affect subordinates. The roots of the transactional style of leadership lie in Theory X management style in which the average adult is seen as lazy, needing to be led, and resistant to change. According to McGregor, both X and Y theories are related to human behavior and rely on how people change to reach organizational goals (Urwick, 1970). A Theory X leader would direct efforts, promote motivation, control actions, and modify behavior of people, and a Theory Y leader would care more for the people factor (Schermerhorn, 2010).

Weiskittel (1999) identified autocratic leadership as the use of commands, expected compliance, power, reward, and punishment. Beinecke and Spencer (2007) described transactional leaders as leaders who accept work within a specific system to maintain the system and the organization. A transactional leader cares for efficiency, planning and goal setting, and competencies. Transactional leadership is the process of using influence and power (Schuster, 1994). The transactional style, which includes a base of trading benefits and implementing a reward–punishment system, reflects the immaturity of leaders in achieving transformational change and a limited (if any) learning opportunity for the constituents (Northouse, 2010).

The bases of transactional leadership lie in the expectancy theory, path-goal theory, exchange–equity theory, reinforcement theory, and maximization orientation (Pearce et al., 2003). Expectancy theory, which is a cognitive-rational model for understanding human behavior, provides an explanation of the method in which individuals evaluate situations according to valence, instrumentality, and expectancy (Bayers, 2004). Under equity theory, transactional leaders use the reward system to achieve maximum motivation among followers (Northouse, 2010).

According to Griffin (2008), the focus of the path-goal theory is how leaders influence the satisfaction and performance of followers by illustrating goals and rewards, which conforms to the transactional nature of leadership. The exchange–equity theory is cognitive-rational in its foundation. The reinforcement theory demonstrates ways in which transactional leaders can reinforce and affect subordinates' desired behaviors through a system of reward. In the Egyptian context, transactional leadership is widely used (Shahin & Wright, 2004).

Transformational theory. Beinecke and Spencer (2007) noted that a transformational leader would care for personal relationships and development. A transformational leader nurtures the organizational culture with empowerment, honesty, humility, teamwork, communication, autonomy and creativity, and continuous learning. Klenke (2002) noted that transforming or transformational leadership is the ability of a leader to transform human conduct through moral exercises. In addition to vision, transformational leaders enjoy charismatic attributes that include ideology, bonds with followers through inspiration and confidence, and powerful auras. To overcome challenges and reach collective interests, leaders attract followers through optimistic and purpose-oriented visions.

Emotional intelligence (EI) is a leader's recognition of his or her own and others' feelings. In coping with environmental demands, EI is the ability to use a diversity of capabilities and competencies to achieve personal goals. According to Klenke (2002), EI includes "self-awareness, self-regulation, empathy, and optimism" (p. 10). Through believability and credibility, leaders are able to build trust with their followers and build collaborative capital. Transformational leaders build culture based on learning and continuous improvement. Reeves (2005) emphasized that through the development of EI, employees can improve personally and professionally. Goleman (2004) emphasized that an organization promoting leadership through EI should give the right information, guidance, and support.

The personal skills once referred to as soft, including self-awareness, relationship management, communication, and social awareness, are becoming the basic required skills for effective team leaders ("Beautiful Minds: Think EQ Not IQ,"2004). Drury and Kitsopoulos (2005) emphasized that EI is not a genetic trait. EI refers to the ability to manage and express feelings appropriately and effectively. People gain EI through a continuous learning process throughout life. The core qualities of EI include initiative, adaptability, resilience, and optimism.

Transformational leadership reflects a leader's involvement not just in coordinating but also in integrating activities (Weiskittel, 1999). According to Conger (1999), transformational leaders assist their followers to realize higher performance outcomes exceeding expectations. Transformational leaders help their followers to adopt new vision and possibilities to create change and opportunities for growth and learning. To inspire and motivate followers, Shahin and Wright (2004) explained that transformational leaders can continue to use authority and power.

Transformational leadership reveals how far a leader is able to develop the inner quest, personal credibility, and other values and skills, beginning with a visible realization of self-awareness. According to Krishnan (2001), transformational leaders have purpose-in-life, strong personal efficacy, emotional and social intelligence, and a value system. The tone and standards of an organization are set by the leader's values, beliefs, vision, and action. Bass (as cited in Banerji & Krishnan, 2000) explained how transformational leaders' behavior can be charismatic, inspirational, intellectually stimulating, and individualized.

Avolio, Bass, and Jung (1999) found that transformational leadership incorporates motivation, shared vision, and challenging experiences. Banerji and Krishnan (2000) noted as the practice of transforming leadership increases, the level of human performance and the ethical determination of both leaders and followers increase in a moral way. Transformational leadership is the energy transmitted by a leader to his or her followers, challenging followers to go through a transformation process to reach identified goals. Transformation is not an easy step because it embodies change in many different ways, including a change of behavior on the personal and organizational levels. Tucker and Russell (2004) explained that transformational leaders provide new direction, inspiration, and behaviors; appeal to higher standards and moral ideals; define and share a long-term vision; and form a base of reliability in the organization and with followers.

Based on the work of Avolio et al. (1999), themes of transformational leadership were identified as examining assumptions, promoting innovative thinking, and focusing on follower development. Leaders need to go through personal transformation before they can contribute to transforming others. Using authority and power, Tucker and Russell (2004) expressed how transformational leaders could be successful in inspiring followers to trust and follow leaders' paths. Transformational leaders affect the organizational culture and the change process through a continuous process of learning, growing, and finding innovations. According to Heifetz and Laurie (2003), the work of leadership includes "getting on the balcony, identifying the adaptive challenge, regulating distress, maintaining disciplined attention, giving the work back to people, and protecting voices of leadership from below" (p. 2). Although the research study did not involve the promotion of a specific leadership type, transformational leadership is discussed further in Chapter 5.

Servant theory. Libby et al. (2006) noted the focus of servant leadership is on values such as dependability, integrity, and fairness. Success is based on the group's hard work, support, and commitment. Servant leadership combines individual traits and collective processes. With a focus on the community level, Headington (2001) noted that servant leaders care to be involved for change. Servant leaders commit to the *we* rather than the *I* concept. Servant leaders focus on people's needs. Rogers and Shriberg (2002) noted servant leaders lead change through changing self, motivating others, developing leaders among followers, and searching for wholeness. Servant leaders are created to satisfy the needs of their communities and people. In the Egyptian context, servant leaders are usually spiritual leaders (Russell, 2003).

Other theories. Leadership studies included other theories that focused on specific themes such as gender (e.g., eomen), introduced interactive methodologies (e.g., adaptive), and explained self-management (e.g., empowering). The next section includes an explanation of a number of additional leadership theories. The additional leadership theories are not age-oriented.

Adaptive leadership. Heifetz's framework for adaptive leadership suggested pedagogical tools for teaching leadership, distinguished between leadership and authority, and differentiated between adaptive and technical challenges (Klau, 2006). Heifetz's adaptive leadership framework introduced the use of interactive methodology based on case-in-point learning, below-the-neck learning, and reflective practice. The basis of the adaptive leadership approach is real-life situations and authentic nature. Through deep educational experiences and self-reflection, adaptive leadership combines adequate emotions and intellect exercises. Adaptive leadership may be used for youth leadership development through diversified learning opportunities and personal choices. Pedagogical tools might include, but are not limited to, lectures, expert panel, evaluation and selection, reflective practice, case-in-point learning, large-group discussion, small-group discussion, community service activity, field trip, cheering, material reward, problem-solving activity, committee activity, religious test study, out-of-context programming, preprogram activities, and follow-up activities. In the Egyptian context, public administration reforms toward decentralization in the past decade have experienced adaptive leadership models (Sayed, 2004).

Empowering leadership. Empowering leadership is the process of leaders developing followers' self-management or self-leadership.

Empowering leadership involves relying on behavioral self-management and social cognitive theory. Self-management theory includes a focus on self through the context of observation, goal setting, reward, punishment, and rehearsal. Social cognitive theory includes a reliance on how leaders' modeling influences subordinates. Spreitzer and Quinn (2003) noted that five disciplines for leadership could be developed through empowerment. The five disciplines are self-empowerment, continuous vision and challenge, security and support, openness and trust, and guidance and control. Through empowerment, leaders develop followers' self-management or self-leadership skills. In the Egyptian context, empowerment leadership was applied with specific groups such as women and youth (IREX, 2010).

Task-oriented leadership. Park (1997) explained that task-oriented leadership style includes behavioral attitude assuming that managers and leaders are the key responsible factors for efficient use of human and capital resources in achieving organizational goals. Leaders are concerned with identifying subordinates' roles, directing, planning, co-coordinating, and problem solving. Task-oriented leaders usually believe in the need to criticize poor work and to pressure subordinates to perform better. Through professional experience, a leader has to do groundwork by identifying basic roles of subordinates. The leader has to be willing and have the authority to intervene in the process if needed. Park highlighted ways in which a relations-oriented leadership style includes different behaviors. In relation- or people-oriented leadership, leaders are supportive, friendly, and considerate. Leaders usually consult with subordinates, represent their interests, are open to communication, and recognize contributions of subordinates. In the Egyptian context, task-oriented leadership has been studied for its application in specific industries such as construction (Abdelhaleem & Seymour, 1994).

Women's leadership. In management and leadership literature, many writers have focused on gender-stereotypical differences in problem solving, decision making, and organizing and processing information. Stereotypic thinking motivated many researchers to challenge the reality of gender differences and the debate that women could execute managerial tasks just as successfully as men if given the right conditions and situation. Buttner (as cited in Hayes, Allinson, & Armstrong, 2004) contended that although research on women's leadership has shown that both genders lead in the same way, their leadership style is affected by gender factors. Other researchers illustrated that feminine characteristics applied a cognitive style and a holistic approach to female leadership. Many feminist writers started to emphasize women's differences through values, ways of behaving, and ways of feeling (Klenke, 2002). In feminists' views, female leaders promote involvement, teamwork, designation and information, and power sharing. For corporate effectiveness, Kark (2004) expressed that women's ways of leading, social skills, and spontaneous mode of thinking should not be seen as disadvantages.

Academic research revealed that no difference exists between the sexes in communication behaviors, leadership style, and sociability (Reeder, 2005). In terms of intuition orientation, Hayes et al. (2004) found that no difference exists between female and male managers. Drury and Kitsopoulos (2005) also noted that no differences exist between the level of EI in men, who tend to be more optimistic, adaptive, and self-confident, and in women, who are more empathic and aware of their emotions.

Park (1997) explained that women have certain qualities that promote a confused understanding about their tendency to adopt feminine or relations-oriented leadership, if any. Park suggested an androgynous leadership style that is integrative rather than polarized. An individual can be a leader because of his or her style, position, and behaviors (Black & Magnuson, 2005). Black and Magnuson (2005) noted how usual literature illustrating women's characteristics conflicted with leadership characteristics.

In comparison to men, Bass (as cited in Hayes et al., 2004) showed that women illustrated higher levels of transformational leadership. For Bass, the transformational leader inspires followers to reach beyond expectations, work on transcendental planes, and achieve collective goals. Research on transformational leadership and gender is still limited. Kark (2004) noted researchers need to look into the gender issue from a wider perspective, including the social system, a new understanding of transformational leadership, and the multifactor research environment. Women may be creating a new leadership paradigm that would be more adjustable to a diverse workplace with a focus on sharing information, collaboration, and teamwork ("Women Leaders More Persuasive," 2005). In the Egyptian context, women's leadership is practiced through local and international nongovernmental organizations in the areas of peace, human trafficking, and youth (The Suzanne Mubarak Women's International Peace Movement, 2010).

Leadership Development: Competencies

A competency is the quality of being competent, which is having the necessary ability or knowledge to do something successful (*American Heritage Dictionary of the English Language*, 2000). Competency is being adequately qualified both physically and intellectually. Tubbs and Schulz (2006) described competencies by the acronym KSA, which is knowledge, skills, and abilities. Competency refers to characteristics leading to the success of a job or a task (Tubbs & Jablokow, 2009). Competencies have two basic levels: technical and behavioral (BC Assessment, 2009). The technical level refers to technical knowledge and skills. The second level refers to behavioral competencies, which relate to how an individual approaches his or her work (e.g., communication, teamwork, and so forth). Key competencies need to be observable, measurable, future oriented, and linked to performance. According to Hoffman (1999), a competency can refer to either an outcome or an input.

Historical overview. Leadership learning should not be limited to classroom setting. Greenberg-Walt and Robertson (2001) suggested that leadership development should be based on experience and observation. Klenke (2002) referred to the influence of context or culture in which leadership flourishes and is practiced. Context affects leaders' perspective, values, and future contributions. In some situations, even a negative context can be the driver for leaders to change their current context and status through positive intervention. Transforming and transformational leadership, EI, and the ability to build trust are leadership competencies connecting context and outcomes (Klenke, 2002). A competent leader needs to master a set of skills, including modeling, inspiring, challenging, enabling, and encouraging

(Kouzes & Posner, 2002). The most valuable competency for a leader's success is the ability to work with others (Kouzes & Posner, 2002).

A leadership competency model needs to include five pillars of "self-management, leading others, task management, innovation, and social responsibility" (Central Michigan University, 2004, p. 5). Self-management includes learning, self-insight, work habits, work attitudes, and stress management. Leading others includes communication, developing others, influencing, motivating others, and interpersonal awareness. Task management includes solving problems, enhancing performance, executing tasks, managing human resources, and managing information and resources. Innovation includes creativity, enterprise, forecasting, managing change, and integrating perspectives. Social responsibility includes acting with integrity, civic responsibility, ethical processes, leading others ethically, and social knowledge.

Clawson (2008) added that leaders need three clusters of skills and abilities to become competent: developing a vision, committing to the developed vision, and monitoring and managing progress to realize that vision. Bolden and Gosling (2006) referred to the development of the leadership competency approach employing behavioral, managerial, and organizational competencies. The competency approach is more complex and focused on outcomes than on behaviors. With the mentioned paradigm shift, competencies are including more interpersonal skills.

Tubbs and Schulz (2006) contributed to leadership research and identified a matrix of leadership competencies and metacompetencies. Tubbs and Schulz also clarified which individual leadership attributes can be developed. Other attributes (personality and values) are more likely fixed at a relatively early age of life. Future research needs to concentrate on prioritizing needed leadership competencies according to various situations (Tubbs & Schulz, 2006). Metacompetencies include the ability to understand the big picture, consider attitudes as everything, see leadership as the driving force, regard communication as the leader's voice, value innovation and creativity, lead change, adopt teamwork, and consider fellowship.

Beinecke and Spencer (2007) concluded that core leadership competencies are universal among careers and countries. Core leadership competencies include a mix of adequate knowledge and interpersonal, transactional, and transformational skills. In a quantitative, cross-sectional study to explore the long-lasting effects on youths' self-esteem, Minor (2007) identified "intelligence, school performance, self-efficiency, stress management, and reaction to peer pressure" (p. 24) as competency factors. The current research study was expected to explore the leadership competencies for youth ages 15–24. At the end of Chapter 5, the study contains a model for needed competencies that can help in developing and implementing effective processes and evaluative methods in programs promoting youth leadership. The listed competencies were also used as themes in the analysis of Round 1 of the study.

Current theories. Brockman et al. (2007) identified core competencies for youth and leadership development as interaction, cooperation, uniqueness, professionalism, and project management. Under interaction, youth need to be competent in debate skills, public speaking and writing, and participation. Conner and Strobel (2007) noted that youth leadership requires competency in communication and interpersonal skills. Under cooperation, youth need to be competent in respecting others, achieving tasks of leader and follower, capitalizing on strengths, and pledging to freedom of group input and expression. Under uniqueness, youth need to be competent in understanding the interactive relationship with the community, belonging as a member to a larger group, realizing areas for self-improvement, and being responsible for actions and the consequences. Under professionalism, youth need to be competent in showing tactfulness, using appropriate protocols and dress, considering context, producing quality work, and positively selling oneself. Under project management, youth need to be competent in goal setting, action planning, facilitating and reflecting, and balancing between individual and community needs.

The study was expected to suggest additional competencies related to entrepreneurship, innovation, and information communication technology. Both the developed and the developing worlds are experiencing the Internet era. The Internet is among the major factors in recognizing a nation's distinction and is considered the hope in crossing the gap and digital divide and finding a unifying way for development and progression between the North and the South hemispheres (Festa, 2003). Ross and Schulz (1999) commented on how the Internet has changed lives and revolutionized many fields, including education. As a venue, online environments are rapidly expanding for learning and teaching in different fields, including education and industry (Vrasidas & Zembylas, 2004). For reaching a wide range of learning outcomes, Prince and Felder (2006) noted how inductive methods, which include "inquiry learning, problem-based learning, project-based learning, case-based teaching, discovery learning, and just-in-time teaching" (p. 1), are more effective than traditional deductive methods. To make instruction motivating, Cao (2005) noted that educators use inclusion, entertainment, and edification in a flexible manner and at the appropriate time.

In addition to the necessary skills and competencies, the training and preparation for future leaders should include the global concept. The work world will need new leaders who are capable of fostering growth, being global, thinking like the customer, being complete leaders, working with processes, being boundary-less, and managing virtually (Krupp & O'Neill, 2007). Future leaders will need to be more entrepreneur-like, intuitive, multicultural, multilingual, and flexible. According to Henderson, Whitaker, Bialeschki, Scanlin, and Thurber (2007), healthy and positive development in youth includes internal and external assets. The internal assets include motivation to learn, values, identity, and interpersonal skills (Henderson et al., 2007). The external assets include effective use of time, limitations and expectations, empowerment, and support.

According to Herzog (2007), by becoming more competent and competitive, future leaders need to develop both intrapersonal and interpersonal relationships. To become whole leaders, future leaders need to consider competencies and skills through a paradigm of complexity, diversity, and uncertainty. The paradigm needs to have levels for competencies. The first level can include developing an international mind-set, cherishing diversity, and considering global responsibility. The second level can include caring for the broader picture, managing creatively, and balancing paradoxes. The highest level is the third level, which is about articulating a point of view, leading teams, and leading change (Henderson et al., 2007).

To view the world and be able to solve problems, Gunter, Estes, and Schwab (2003) noted that educators should increase complex mental organization and students' dynamic interaction with surrounding stimulations. Youth need exposure to a variety of learning opportunities and diversified channels for experiencing leadership. With regard to education, Marsh and Willis (2003) noted curriculum developers should have extensive experience and knowledge about the subject matter, pedagogy, curriculum design, evaluation, organization, and writing. Gong (2005) reported how critical thinking is related to fairness, and objectivity. In addition to critical thinking, curriculum designers should consider integration of values. With a more balanced and updated curriculum, education might be an effective partner in youth leadership development.

With regard to civil participation, Vigilante (2003) suggested that to develop responsible and active citizens and a society of stakeholders, leaders of any nation need to care for the investment in education and open a culture of democracy. Leaders need to encourage educated citizens to access and use information in political participation and life usages. Klau (2006) described a research study conducted by the Carnegie Foundation in the United States over a 10-year period. Results of the study indicated youth leadership education was disconnected from youth needs. Most studies and organizations serving youth are implicit and fail to examine ideas about youth trait leadership development.

Bolden and Gosling (2006) contended that adopting a competency approach is a repeated refrain with a narrow focus on the leader as an individual rather than on leadership as a distributed relational process. The research study identified leadership competencies, processes, and evaluative tools for enforcing leadership as a relational process to build effective leadership programs for youth ages 15–24.

Leadership Development: Process

Libby et al. (2006) noted how youth leadership development is considered a new discipline of study. MacNeil (2006) explained how considerable literature is related to adult leadership and limited consideration for youth leadership. Kress (2006) referred to the definition of leadership in *Webster's Collegiate Dictionary* as one's authority or influence to direct the operation, activity, or performance of others. Leadership necessitates the presence of marginal advantage or superiority. Successful leaders are expected to have the following characteristics: knowledge, competency, and character. Leaders' tools for leadership include reflective learning, interaction, decision making, motivation, and other skills contributing to effective action. Leskiw and Singh (2007) recommended six essential factors for effective leadership development: needs assessment, selection of proper audience, design of apt infrastructure, learning system, an evaluation system, and rewarding success and improving deficiencies.

Historical overview. Many programs and opportunities contributing to youth leadership were labeled as character development, life preparations, building relationships, and community (Libby et al., 2006). Youth leadership development must include youth empowerment with values, power, and action. Youth leadership opportunities are generated through a theory of change (Libby et al., 2006). To promote effective youth leadership processes through an ontological reality, Guajardo (2002) noted that societies should follow a new political practice in which they conceive of young people as active and place youth in the center of the educational policy. Saunders (2002) concluded that youth leadership programming should incorporate a youth-oriented approach to education and perspectives on leadership.

Researchers at the Organisation for Economic Co-operation and Development (OECD) suggested a framework for key competencies that should be targeted toward success for individuals and society. For effective youth development with a leadership competency base, OECD (2005) researchers called for a movement beyond knowledge and skills. Young leaders are expected to be adaptive, innovative, self-motivated, and initiator. In addition to the ability to mobilize cognitive and practical abilities, young leaders' programs need to adopt a reflective system for thoughts and actions and consider combining key competencies according to context. Key competencies can be classified under three categories: using tools effectively, working cooperatively in diverse groups, and acting independently (OECD, 2005). The first category includes the use of language, symbols, text, knowledge, information, and technology. The second category involves relating well to others, cooperating, managing, and resolving conflicts. The third category includes acting through the big picture; developing personal projects and life plans; and asserting rights, interests, needs, and limits.

In addition to competency development, youth leadership development must consider self-efficacy. Self-efficacy is one's belief about his or her capabilities to achieve a target. Self-efficacy has consequences and influences in all aspects of life. Margolis and McCabe (2006) realized how low self-efficacy beliefs can affect academic achievement and create psychological devastation through a continuous sense of failure and learned helplessness. Schunk (2004) defined self-efficacy as the personal awareness of potential capabilities and associated actions. Self-efficacy affects students' readiness to take on more tasks, learn, and succeed. Self-efficacy, which is the hidden force for belief, is a vital reason for self-concept, self-realization, self-image, and self-confidence.

Best practices. Some examples of best practices of youth organizations or organizations focused on youth leadership development in Africa, the Middle East region, and some developed countries follow. The selection was not easy, especially with developed countries, because of the large number of examples of best practices and a long history of their existence and experiences.

Africa. In Africa, most programs on youth leadership development are for youth ages 25–45 with a focus on entrepreneurship, work skills, and peace (Communication Initiative Network, 2004; Leap Africa, 2009; Mihyo & Ogbu, 2000). The listed programs are mainly funded by international funding organizations such as Ford Foundation, U.S. Agency for International Development, and International Development Research Center. The programs varied between East and West African countries. The African Leadership

Academy (ALA, 2010) is among the very few listings of organizations that had a focus similar to the focus within the current study on youth leadership development for youth ages 15–18 years old.

International. Since 1844, the Young Men's Christian Association (YMCA) has been an international, Christian, ecumenical, and voluntary movement for both women and men. YMCA encourages the unique involvement of young people to promote the Christian values through building a human community based on the principles of justice, love, peace and reconciliation (Zurlinden, 2005). To work for social justice, YMCA serves young adults in 125 countries with national movements in Armenia, Australia, Guatemala, Scotland, Sweden, United States, and Zambia. Working toward equitable societies, YMCA's unique methodology is evidenced through empowering young men and women to welcome responsibilities and engage in leadership at different levels without any discrimination based on religion, race, or gender. YMCA is one of the oldest and largest movements in the world with a focus on youth development.

Margolis and McCabe (2006) concluded that belief can change behavior. A good example is the Australian Youth Development Association (AYDA). Through school programs, conferences, and travel, AYDA (2010) has been working with youth in Australia to enhance the self-esteem of young adults and create future leaders. AYDA defined leadership as any action that makes the world's youth touch a better future. AYDA has extended its travel experiences to Africa to give its participants different perspectives about leadership and service. AYDA uses young role models as leadership ambassadors for interactions with their participants to build a sense of self-belief, self-confidence, and self-worth.

Some of the educational initiatives related to youth leadership involved Education for All, promoting cultural heritage, diversity, and peace; accessing vocational training; advancing human rights; promoting enterprise training; and accessing training programs (United Nations, 2004). A number of internationally funded and implemented international programs exist in Egypt; these programs also function in some other countries in the region, with documented impact on youth development and leadership. At the university level, Students in Free Enterprise and the Discovery Program, which is part of the Institute for International Education, exist at a number of public and private universities (Institute of International Education, 2010; Students in Free Enterprise, 2010). At the school level, the International Education and Resource Network (iEARN) and INJAZ, which is part of the Junior Achievement Program, are present through their work with the Ministry of Education (iEARN, 2010; INJAZ, 2010).

Middle East. Located in Sana'a, the capital of Yemen, the Youth Leadership Development Foundation (YLDF) is a nongovernmental and nonprofit organization. YLDF (2010) was originally founded to motivate, support, and develop youth to become part of the decision-making process and development of Yemen. YLDF serves children and youth ages 8–30 years old in a number of areas including language, culture, economic development, management, and leadership training. Although the foundation was established in the late 1990s for girls only, the foundation now welcomes both genders. The mission of YLDF is to make youth more responsive to their community and labor market through increased social, political, and economic participation. YLDF conducts systematic training and education in different fields such as vocational, communication, and leadership.

The section of best practices led to a recommendation for future research to examine if youth leadership programs in international environments are based on similar competencies, whether basic youth leadership programs are portable from country to country, and, if not, what influences the distinctions from country to country. MacNeil (2006) concluded that young people are learning about leadership through many programs, without adequate opportunities for practicing leadership. Practicing leadership is affected by culture, identity, process, procedures, and context of leadership practices.

Current theories. Conner and Strobel (2007) concluded that previous research studies lacked a clear definition of youth leadership competencies and process. MacNeil (2006) emphasized that among the thousands of studies written about leadership, youth leadership was absent. Youth leadership was mentioned in reference to future orientation rather than current practices, deficit models, youth as a resource, and educational contexts.

Libby et al. (2006) noted that research is necessary in the area of effective youth leadership development practices and its components. Horstmeier and Ricketts (2009) highlighted the four levels of leadership contexts, which are self, interpersonal, group and organizations, and community and society. Tubbs and Schulz (2006) noted that leadership consists of a three-level model of attributes including the individual's core personality level, the individual's values, and the individual's leadership behaviors and skills. The outermost level represents the metacompetencies and is the most likely level for change through leadership development.

An individual's personality is his or her reserve of physical and mental attributes causing a unique identity. A personality is shaped due to the continuous interaction between heredity and a person's environment (e.g., cultural, familial, and social; Tubbs & Schulz, 2006). Early intervention with character-building programs and activities assists in leadership potential. According to Tubbs and Schulz (2006), leaders and entrepreneurs are individuals with personalities containing high levels of the personality dimensions, which are extravert, agreeable, conscientious, emotionally stable, and open to experience.

To ensure a strong leadership pipeline, Krupp and O'Neill (2007) suggested that youth leadership service providers need to consider the attraction, development, and retention of leaders. When approaching leadership development, trainers need to consider people's strengths and leverage them, taking into account the whole leader and balancing the development of the head, heart, and guts of the leader (Krupp & O'Neill, 2007). Leadership development approaches should emphasize continuous learning and growing. DuBois, Lockerd, Reach, and Parra (2003) explored the importance of adopting fundamental changes in using curricula-based and didactic approaches to include more experiential and context-based approaches with a focus on community-based initiatives.

On both the individual and the programmatic levels, Conner and Strobel (2007) focused on examining three dimensions: communication competencies, analytical and critical skills, and active involvement in community issues. The focus of youth leadership programs should be on group processes and collective action rather than on approaches of documenting achievements and promotional wording. Leaders of youth leadership programs need to explore leadership theories for youth and their best practices rather than rely only on current theories of leadership, which are primarily for adults.

Jennings et al. (2006) described empowerment as a social action process with a multilevel process including practical approaches and applications on individual and collective levels and outcomes. Critical youth empowerment is a conceptual framework centered on the foundation of integrating youth empowerment processes and outcomes at both the individual and the collective levels. At the individual level, programs need to focus on psychological empowerment. Individuals need to grow through capacity building, personal control, a positive approach to life, and a critical comprehension and sense of the surrounding sociopolitical environment. With regard to collective empowerment, program leaders need to consider carefully the processes and structures that improve youths' skills, provide mutual support and collective well-being, and increase both intra- and inter-organizational networks and bonds to build a strong and effective community life. In Chapter 5, the research results and participants' feedback related to youth leadership processes will be compared to the critical youth empowerment conceptual framework.

According to researchers at the United Nations (2004), youth participation and empowerment can be achieved through equity, equal access to opportunities (education and employment), services (health care), and information. To ensure relevance, efficiency, and effectiveness, participation and empowerment comprise the process of involving youth in youth-related policies, programs, and services through planning, implementation, monitoring, and evaluating. Conceptualizing youth empowerment as a bipolar continuum does not reflect other key dimensions of this complex social action process, such as the philosophy and values underlying youth programs and initiatives, the dynamics of youth–adult relationships within these initiatives, and individual and collective processes of critical reflection and reflective action to address social injustice and inequities. Rissel (1994) emphasized the integrated and sociopolitical dimensions of empowerment, noting,

> Community empowerment includes a raised level of psychological empowerment among its members, a political action component in which members have actively participated, and the achievement of some redistribution of resources or decision making favorable to the community or group in question. (p. 41)

A major factor in youth leadership development is the quality of individuals offering the service (e.g., teachers, caregivers). Huebner, Walker, and McFarland (2003) criticized the status of lacking clear requirements, qualifications, and professional development for the people working with young leaders. Huebner et al. identified a youth development professional as an expert in informal educational and experiential learning settings, and assist young leaders in meeting basic needs, and developing necessary competencies and skills for becoming contributing leaders of communities. Ornstein (1997) commented on how experienced teachers are caring professionals who focus on the students' needs rather than themselves.

Instructional planning is the teachers' responsibility to meet students' needs and make learning attainable. Although Ornstein's (1997) conclusion referred to teachers in the educational field, the same concept can be adjusted and used with youth workers and caregivers in youth development programs. According to Gunter et al. (2003), learners need meaningful learning engagement; direct contact with content; and numerous opportunities to express self and understandings, creative assessment, and evaluation methods.

Effective teachers and youth caregivers need to use their understanding and experience in the utilization of background knowledge, learning styles, multiple intelligences, brain and learning connections, and special needs in planning effective activities for teaching and learning. Teachers are composers who put the curriculum pieces together to create a rhythm to reach the students (Marsh & Willis, 2003). In instructional planning, teachers use all available knowledge, skills, environments, attitudes, and so forth to assist students in learning. Teachers need to plan with a focus on the identity of the students, the nature of their needs, and their goals of education (Martin, 2003).

Educationalists should carefully design instructions linked to intended learning outcomes. Educators should be equipped and ready to use a variety of approaches and techniques to reach planned instructional objectives (Gunter et al., 2003).

Educators should be aware and find appropriate methods of assessment and evaluation to the learning objectives (Huba & Freed, 2000). Assessment and evaluation should be an ongoing procedure through the teaching and learning process. Evaluation involves asking questions and verifying whether teaching and learning match objectives and students are learning (Canton & Hancock, 2007).

Historical overview in Egypt. Due to Egypt's various attempts to offer youth mental, physical, and professional preparation for the future, a number of programs and organizations were created, including the National Council for Youth, Civil Education Center, Youth Parliament, Development of Voluntary Spirit, and Combating Literacy (Egypt State Information Service, 2006b). Due to the large population and limited resources, the above-mentioned programs are not accessible to all youth. Three of Egypt's earlier and current national initiatives in the area of youth leadership development are the Youth Socialism Institute, National Youth Policy, and International Youth Camp.

Youth Socialism Institute. Shokr (2004) concluded that the experience of the Youth Socialism Institute was a result of its own time and environment; policy makers can learn many lessons from the experience. The institute's main factors for developing new young leaders were based on scientific knowledge and awareness and an entrepreneurial spirit based on physical action and a positive relationship with the public. Under the leadership of former president Nasser, the Youth Socialism Institute was developed in 1963 through a realistic, independent, and public movement to create a new generation of young leaders during the 1960s and 1970s. The institute's intellectuals and developers included different ideologies and backgrounds, including Nationalists, Liberals, Islamists, and Marxists. The institute supported five principles: the integration between intellectual development and the practice of leadership skills, leadership development through in-house accommodation in a series of overnight camps, continuous assessment and evaluation of the participants' progress in public activities, integration in the public community work and leadership training, and open discussion and debates to encourage the young leaders' self-expression. The institute recruited secondary and college student members. Through the three levels of leadership development, the institute offered its members 45 lectures to broaden the political, economic, and social awareness of the members. The institute's program also included community development activities and public service. In 1976, former president Sadat demolished the Youth Socialism Institute.

Shokr (2004) interviewed 100 current Egyptian leaders who had joined the Youth Socialism Institute and asked the leaders to reflect on their experience and how the institute had built their leadership skills. Among the 100 interviewed leaders, 50 participants became leaders in the political arena, such as elected presidents of political parties; 48 became elected board members or directors in nongovernmental organizations; 26 became executive directors in governmental organizations, including ministers; 20 became heads of student councils in the 1960s; 18 became elected members in the People's Assembly and Shoura Council; 16 became elected heads in the workers' syndicates; 14 became university professors including deans and university vice presidents; 13 became owners of companies and businesspeople in multidimensional companies and industries; 11 became intellectuals and journalists; and nine became leaders in professional syndicates.

Youth policy. According to the National Democratic Party (2006), youth are the nation's top priority and represent a vital role in Egypt's development. The National Youth Policy makers should consider youth's needs. Based on Egyptian constitutional rights, youth have the right to live, learn, work, and receive cultural, social, and health services. Youth also have the right of protection against discrimination, equality before the law, equal opportunities, freedom of expression, and demonstration, as well as the right to participate in local and national decision making. The National Youth Policy is a declared commitment to young people.

Youth policy should be comprehensive and based upon partnership of significant stakeholders (Youth Partnership, 2005). The policy was tailored to cover areas of youth needs in employability, political and social participation, education, health, culture and media, sports and entertainment, environment, and research studies. A national youth policy should be drafted in "concrete terms, [and] define objectives, strategies, concrete steps, target groups, timeframe, monitoring and evaluation" (Youth Partnership, 2005, p. 7). Assaad and Barsoum (2007) highlighted how the creation of employment for youth is a top priority on the national agenda, referring to the program named Putting Our Youth to Work, which was expected to create 4.5 million jobs between 2005 and 2011 in the fields of industry, agriculture, and tourism.

According to the Policy Project (2005), although Egypt developed various policies related to adolescents, implemented policies and programs are not responding to youth's needs. Official institutions in Egypt are not consistent in using definitions and lack operational coordination. Youth Partnership (2005) noted the problems facing youth policies: a lack of collaboration between stakeholders in youth policies, lack of trust between young people and governmental authorities, and the large unemployment problem facing young adults in Egypt. A number of initiatives toward youth participation in national youth policy are present through funded programs (e.g., Anna Lindh Foundation, 2009). Current results are still limited to trials, and no clear youth policy has been yet identified. Egypt is also trying to catch up with other developments in the region, such as the development of the National Youth Policy in Jordan (UNDP, 2009).

International Youth Camp. With a focus on agricultural and civilization areas, the International Youth Camp was developed by the Egyptian government and welcomes regional and international participation. The camp objectives are for youth to meet and get to know each other; exchange experiences, cultures, and information; use one common language for dialogue; and work collaboratively on the concepts of peace and safety using culture as the basis for and language of peace. The camp included youth-led activities such as tree planting, visiting major cities, listing natural resources, and touring cities in the region where the camp is conducted. The camp was first conducted in 1963 and is under the umbrella of the National Council for Youth. In 2006, the 38th Annual International Youth Camp was held in Nuweiba and Sharm El Sheikh in South Sinai and inaugurated by former first lady Suzanne Mubarak. The camp used to attract hundreds of college-level youth. The main language used was English (International Youth Camp, 2006).

Current theories in Egypt. According to the World Bank (2010), Egypt is among the world's 10th most active reformers. The *Human Development Report for 2007/2008* indicated Egypt's human development index ranked 112th out of 177countries and 48th among 108 developing countries. The Human Development Index includes the country's welfare in relation to living a long and healthy life, being educated, and having a decent living standard (UNDP, 2009).

MacNeil (2006) identified leadership as the ability to combine ability and authority to positively affect and impact various persons and contexts. Leadership is an applied concept based on balanced value between ability and authority of the leader. Leadership development needs to consider skills, experiences, needs, motivation, and cumulative long effort (Kress, 2006). According to Ricketts and Rudd (2002), youth leadership development has three stages: awareness, interaction, and mastery. To be able to recognize youth's optimal zone, youth leadership programs and decision makers should get to know the youth and surrounding environments. Different factors that influence youth and might affect their leadership development (e.g., adolescence, education, political, economic, social, religious, and theoretical factors) were explored.

Adolescence. Van Linden and Fertman (1998) noted the difficulty of generalizing the status among adolescences as they differ in education, experience, personality characteristics, learning styles, status, socioeconomics, ethnicity, and gender. MacNeil (2006) highlighted issues to be addressed as low academic achievement, negative perception about young people, obesity, poverty, and limited resources allocated for youth development. According to the United Nations (2004), the challenges that face youth include limited resources, inequities, gender discrimination, unsafe livelihoods, unemployment, wars and armed conflicts, and poverty. Some of the signs exhibited by children include 130 million are out of school and 133 million are illiterate. Youth represent 41% of the world's unemployment, and 238 million young adults survive on less than $1 per day. Almost 12 million young men and women live with HIV or AIDS.

Klau (2006) noted the change in approaching adolescent development. In past decades, the focus was on delinquency, pathology, and problem prevention. In recent years, more interest has been tailored toward health, opportunity development, and resilience. To promote resiliency, educators, policy makers, youth workers, and psychologists need to explore factors related to support systems (family, peer, and social), values, aspirations, self-awareness, motivation to succeed, and initiation (Klau, 2006).

According to Martin (2003), students' internal motivation is affected by boosters and guzzlers. The boosters promote self-belief, continuous learning, importance of schooling, determination, study management, planning, and monitoring. The guzzlers encourage anxiety, minimal control, failure avoidance, and self-handicapping. Students are influenced by external motivational factors such as parental engagement; a positive, supportive school environment; student-centered teaching and learning pedagogy; diversified extracurricular activities; student engagement in school governance; community development; offerings of encouragement and praise; and clarity of school policies and regulations. In considering youth leadership development, adults need to understand and realize the challenges adolescence experience, including emotional, physical, and intellectual changes (Oyserman, 2001). In the current study, the sample included youth (19–24 years old) as one the major stakeholders in youth leadership development.

Education. Education is a human right (Hancook, 2005). Not all children have the same access or quality of education because of schools' environment, local and federal funding, parental choice, and so forth. According to the United Nations Educational, Scientific and Cultural Organization (2006), the Egyptian educational system is one of the largest systems in the world. With more than 90 percent enrollment in public schools, the pre-university Egyptian educational system includes more than 15.5

million students, 800,000 educators, and 35,000 schools. In addition to the family's protective and authoritarian mode, the Egyptian educational system is not helping children and youth to develop basic competencies and skills toward leadership and life skills (e.g., critical thinking, problem solving, and so forth). Gunter et al. (2003) noted developing critical thinking can be problematic if the curriculum is strongly content oriented.

Because of recent major educational initiatives, Egypt has achieved quantitative improvements rather than improving the quality of educational services (Vigilante, 2003). The State University (2009) noted how the educational system in Egypt has been affected by the different political tides and economic changes. The Egyptian national curriculum remains tailored toward producing students in the socialist regime of the last century. The curriculum is not student centered and does not promote inquiry, critical skills, and character building. The methods of instruction mainly include the lecture style of teaching with no encouragement of student participation or expression (Hargreaves, 1997). Instruction is still affected by the social and cultural heritage (i.e., youngsters do not debate or argue and self-expression is selfish and egoistic).

In schools and learning environments, students should have basic rights such as learning, equal opportunity and nondiscrimination, freedom of speech, privacy, and a safe and healthy school environment (Essex, 2005). Students are to be accountable for their behavior, to assist school management in drafting school policies, and to be active members in the school and community by enforcing the law and policies (Jazzar & Algozzine, 2006). The educational systems in Egypt and the MENA region are geared to prepare young adults to serve in the public sector and do not help in the school-to-work transition (Assaad & Roudi-Fahimi, 2007). Current educational systems widen the gap between needs of the new enterprises and human skills.

Since 1990, a number of collaborative initiatives have been ongoing with donor agencies to advance educational reform. Among the many initiatives, Egypt worked on Education for All, Education for Excellence and Excellence for All, and developing national standards for education (Ministry of Education, 2010). According to the World Bank (2008), middle-performing countries such as Egypt have a unique mix of educational achievements and challenges. Egypt has universal primary education and reduced the gender gap at all levels of education (UNDP, 2009). As a challenge, educational reform needs to consider seriously the issues of high literacy levels and quality of education. Educational reformers need to adopt modern pedagogical methods integrating inquiry-based learning and teaching to the students' individual learning capacity (Galal, 2008). Global, regional, and local economic needs necessitate the production of well-educated, technically skilled graduates who are ready for joining the workforce, capable of adopting new technologies, proficient in new sets of transversal skills, and competent in foreign languages and science training.

Political. Until the middle of the 20th century, Egypt had a number of young political leaders who proved to be well-trained to rule and who influenced the region and the world. A few examples are King Tut, Queen Hatshepsout, King Farouk, and President Nasser. In 1954, President Nasser ruled the country at the age of 36 (Khalil, 2002). Under the Nasser regime, Egypt was trying to develop a cadre of young political leaders who were capable of envisioning the future and assisting Egypt to overcome its challenges (Shokr, 2004). Although Nasser's era was mainly socialist, the initiative successfully brought together experts and nationalists from different backgrounds and ideologies.

Researchers at Koinonia House (2009) noted the Egyptian political system is characterized as a socialist dictatorship. To maintain the status quo, the current political system has oppressed any leadership traits within the single ruling party or other opposing elements. Libby et al. (2006) commented, "Young people have often been targeted by oppressive rhetoric and policies and scapegoated for social ills" (p. 17). Farag (2007) made a connection between what took place in Egypt's university youth demonstrations in 1977 and what is taking place in the 21st century. Youth demonstrations and rebellious movements reflect societal suffering from economic and social ills. The forceful reaction of the government at that time was well learned by parents and subsequent generations. The tragic incident led to less political, economic, and social actions by youth.

Economic. Saad Eddin (1996) explained that overpopulation, scarcity of resources, reduced productivity, inadequate government bureaucracy, and increasing foreign-debt load comprise Egypt's ills. In addition to a growing population, Egypt suffers from low and unfair income distribution (less than $6,000 per capita) and lack of equity (Central Intelligence Agency, 2010). In 2006, Egypt's population reached 72.58 million (American Chamber of Commerce in Egypt, 2007). Deficient economic planning and decision making have become deeply rooted due to a lack of suitable leadership skills among governmental agencies and personnel (Sayed, 2004).

Van Linden and Fertman (1998) ranked the employers' rating of new hire skills in relationship to leadership as teamwork, interpersonal skills, verbal and written communication, computer skills, analytical skills, and leadership skills. The same employers rated leadership as fourth among 10 needed skills for new hires. For career and societal success, educational systems should consider leadership development among its formal programming to avoid limiting leadership opportunity to students or youth who are only involved in extracurricular activities and youth organizations. Similar to the study by Van Linden and Fertman, researchers at the Egyptian International Economic Forum (2009) conducted a research study to explore work competencies needed in the private sector. The study was only run among the forum's members, and the results were not publicized.

On a global leadership level, Krupp and O'Neill (2007) noted the gap between current leadership capabilities and the emerging business requirements and future demands. Many employers and leadership programs have been traditional in their offering and teaching rather than focusing on what is needed for the future. Assaad and Roudi-Fahimi (2007) commented on how current circumstances happening inside and outside the MENA region affects its youth, such as the use of the Internet, globalization, and financial crises. The MENA region is witnessing significant differences compared to other world regions in youth unemployment rates, gender gaps, illiteracy rates, and population growth.

Social. Arab families, who are overprotective parents, use an authoritarian mode in child rearing (UNDP, 2003). Authoritarian child rearing negatively influences children's independence, decision-making, self-confidence, and social efficiency. The way children are raised and treated in Arab countries, including Egypt, negatively affects children's natural interest in questioning, exploring, and taking initiative. In Egypt, parents and communities do not encourage self-expression, choices, and uniqueness (UNDP, 2010).

Parents play a major role in shaping children's lives. Responsible parenting includes encouraging youth's growth and experiences outside the home and under the guidance of other adults (Henderson et al., 2007). Due to biased traditions, many parents do not encourage their children, especially girls, to experience opportunities outside their home (Forsythe, Korzeniewicz, Majid, Weathers, & Durrant, 2003). Because of the high value placed on education, Falola and Lerner (2004) noted Egyptian parents discourage activities that would distract children and youth from studying.

Mitra (2005) described the concept of community of practice, which determines the relationship between adults and youth on an equal and partnership basis through mutual engagement. To fulfill the group's goals and objectives, roles are distributed based on capabilities, talents, and perspectives. The group needs to have a group culture derived from a common set of skills, language, and norms. El Issawy (2005) warned future leaders that teamwork is limited in Egypt due to factors related to finances, politics, social readiness, teamwork value, and time.

Religious. Nations have struggled with the value of religion. Many have given religion full importance and have become a one-religion nation. Others have tried to contribute to the benefits of diversity by developing secular nations. Egypt is struggling between the two poles. Mirza (2002) commented on how societies (including culture and individuals) suffer when religion attain overwhelming social power. According to the Council for Secular Humanism (2008), secular humanism is defined as a lifestyle and understanding that rejects supernatural and authoritarian beliefs. Secularism calls for individual responsibility for one's own life, the community, and the world; logical reasoning and scientific investigation; personal freedom and responsibility; human ethics; and tolerance and collaboration. Egypt is a secular country with a majority Muslim population (Egypt State Information Service, 2010). Many civil laws and social practices are affected by Sharia (Islamic code). Schools and the national curriculum are also part of the recent overwhelming religious influence, and all students learn Quran verses for Arabic literacy and poetry classes. To have a proper secular identity, the curriculum should be balanced and include references to other religions.

Mawdsley (2002) questioned if the practice of restricting religious practices would lead to the possibility of a more hostile environment in the school instead of building an environment of diversity. In Egypt, religion is a major component of the character building of any child. In recent years and due to low economic standards, many youth have been diverted toward extreme views in their religions. Both Muslim and Christian extremist groups (inside and outside Egypt) found the status of youth as an opportunity for recruitment for terrorist activities. The extremist groups' financial generosity arising from their understanding of the youth's needs (i.e., marriage, employment, housing, and so forth) has accelerated the process of youth recruitment.

Hopkins and Saad (2004) explained how the spread of the religious extremist movement corresponded with the unique governmental expansion and bureaucratization of the Islamic institutions in the region. Sparre and Petersen (2007) referred to the growing religious movements through youth organizations for social change. The youth movements help participating young adults to gain skills in argumentation techniques, critical thinking, and teamwork. One of the governmental fears was how these movements might transform youth into formal political actors.

Leadership Development: Evaluation

Evaluation methodology and theory have evolved since the 1960s to ensure governmental accountability, especially in the health services and spending in the United States. At first, evaluation practices were limited to quantitative methods. Over the years, evaluation was extended to qualitative methods as well. Most evaluation approaches and practices involve stakeholders in the planning and conduct of the evaluation (Michie, 2001). In the current research study, invited Delphi experts participated in a series of questionnaires and provided controlled feedback to reach group consensus regarding needed competencies, processes, and evaluative tools for developing effective youth leadership programs for youth ages 15–24 in Egypt in the future.

Historical overview. Powell (2006) noted evaluation should be a rigorous and systematic process used to assist in gaining knowledge, making decisions, and implementing practical applications. The evaluation process can be used to evaluate services, programs, processes, personnel, organizations, and resources. Evaluation methods include "input measurement, output/performance measurement, impact/ outcomes assessment, service quality assessment, process evaluation, benchmarking, standards, quantitative methods, qualitative methods, cost analysis, organizational effectiveness, program evaluation methods, and LIS-centered methods" (Powell, 2006, p. 102).

Evaluation has two main types: outcome and process evaluations (Wholey, Hatry, & Newcomer, 2004). The focus of outcome evaluations is cause and effect. The focus of process evaluations is inputs. Other evaluations are related to cost-effectiveness or value for money (Canton & Hancock, 2007). Evaluation has two forms: formative and summative. For the formative evaluation, Gordon (2004) cautioned educational administrators not to be dependent on checklists of non measurable knowledge areas, performance, and dispositions. The promotion of rational models of pedagogical development and integration of various affecting factors are needed. Marsh and Willis (2003) noted how summative evaluation is focused on data that determines the level to which students have attained the final outcomes of the curriculum. Marsh and Willis added that a number of evaluative models are available, including the objective, countenance, illuminative and educational connoisseurship models.

Effective evaluation is based on careful planning early in the design stage to ensure the research questions are answered (Canton & Hancock, 2007). Evaluation should involve looking closely at objectives of the study, program or method to be evaluated, evaluation method, sample, data to be collected, data analysis, and finally dissemination of the results. For evaluative purposes, a useful rubric should contain levels of mastery, dimension of quality, organizational grouping, commentaries, and description of consequences (Huba & Freed, 2000).

Current theories. In addition to evaluating youth leadership programs, evaluation can be an approach or a model for achieving youth leadership. Libby et al. (2006) described three models for youth participation in setting community needs, resolving problems, and making decisions. The three models are youth philanthropy, evaluation and action research, and policy advocacy.

For sustainability, Libby et al. (2006) reported that youth leadership development has to consider inside and outside paths, top-down and grassroots approach, and science-based strategies. Through a case study conducted over 3 years, Conner and Strobel (2007) found that youth have a role in shaping the same developmental context that shaped them. Based upon the research findings, Conner and Strobel verified the dialogical effect of youth developmental programs in affecting youth and being affected by youth. Conner and Strobel noted how the four stakeholder groups agreed to consider creating youth-friendly environments, encouraging youth leadership opportunities, increasing channels for life skills practice, and supporting character building. Brown Urban (2008) conducted an exploratory study to identify youth development components and characteristics through a community-based participatory approach among policy makers, practitioners, researchers, and youth.

Conclusion

While much research has been conducted on leadership for adults and organizations, a thorough review of the literature revealed no studies directly addressed youth leadership, leadership competencies for youth (ages 15–24), process of youth leadership development, or effective tools for youth leadership programs in an Egyptian context. No Delphi studies were found on leadership programs in Egypt. Harrison (1999) noted how current leadership practices are no closer to an understanding than those in early stages. The contemporary confusion regarding leadership is mainly about how leadership was studied in the past. Leadership was also considered in an industrial worldview. Humankind is challenged not by understanding leadership concepts and theories, but by applying it in everyday situations. Wilson (2006) concluded personal and professional life experiences can influence the development of leaders' competencies. Many questions are raised related to the process of leadership development and its outcomes. The results of the study overcame the contradiction and deficiency of knowledge about leadership as a process, especially for youth ages 15–24, through group consensus across different stakeholders in the field of adolescence and youth leadership.

Leadership and especially youth leadership still need to be studied. G. Clark (2001) noted how leadership continues to be mysterious, intangible, and least implicit academic disciplines. Horstmeier and Ricketts (2009) explained that youth's role in society is affected by the spectrum of adults' perception of youth. The spectrum ranges from youth as objects, recipients, resources, and partners. In the research study, stakeholders were asked about previous experiences with leadership and future anticipation of needed competencies, processes, and evaluative tools to develop youth leadership programs.

Leadership skills and capacities are not universal. Conner and Strobel (2007) suggested that leadership development programs need to introduce different skills and capacities among leaders, consider the amount of time needed, encourage positive reinforcement and continuous reflection, support goal setting, and balance opportunities for growth with interaction with adults. The study filled the gap of knowledge between what researchers and educators have reached so far and what needs to be learned and practiced in the area of leadership and specifically youth leadership and development.

Youth development is the process of considering the whole young person. Edelman, Gill, Comerford, Larson, and Hare (2004) explained how youth development became the process or approach to develop or become competent to overcome challenges and be successful. The needed competencies include "cognitive, social, civic, cultural, spiritual, vocational, physical, emotional, mental, personal, moral, or intellectual development"

(Edelman et al., 2004, p. 8). Youth leadership is part of the youth development process. Youth leadership focuses on mastering certain competencies such as vision, responsibility, and collaboration. A review of the literature revealed no consensus on needed competencies for youth leaders. Miller (2008) noted that youth leadership can be classified under leadership qualities, vision, shared leadership, and coaching and training. Competencies can be driven from the different classifications based on need, culture, and context. Through the gaps of knowledge about competencies for young leaders, answering RQ1 involved exploring needed competencies for young leaders ages 15–24 and the responses contributed to the body of knowledge in leadership studies.

The findings of the literature review revealed that even though different leadership models developed over a continuum of time and needed decades and centuries to evolve, common ground was found. First, leadership was always seen as a relationship (Column, 2003). Leadership understanding, use, nature, importance, and direction were identified as common factors among models. Second, leadership was never considered in a vacuum; all other factors, including culture, scarce resources, and outcomes, were considered (Furash, 2003). Third, leadership was a cumulative effort (Kress, 2006). Leadership research and understanding evolved through learned lessons and earlier theories (House, 1996). Leadership understanding and process development is an ongoing process (Day, 2000). The current study involved examining the learned lessons about leadership in Egypt and other countries and knowledge gaps found through the research questions. As an example, answering RQ2 involved exploring effective processes to develop leadership for young leaders aged 15–24 in Egypt.

Wren (2004) illustrated the path of many leaders throughout ancient civilizations and showed how contemporary leadership has been affected. Through the path of leadership, leaders have gained insights, roots, and origins of stories and compiled a massive number of learned lessons and experiences. Wren noted that culture is the sum of community heritage, and humanly transmitted traits through the economic, social, and political forms. Based on

Wren's conclusion about cultural effects, the research study included leadership theories tailored to align with the Egyptian culture and context.

Based on the distinction between forceful and enabling leadership, and locus of power and action, Kaplan and Kaiser (2003) described two dimensions of human nature and leadership. The two dimensions are "autocratic and participative, initiating structure and consideration, self-assertive and empowering, task-oriented and people-oriented" (Kaplan & Kaiser, 2003, p. 15). Bolman and Deal (2003) noted how wise leaders are aware of their own strengths, able to expand them, and develop teams that can become leaders in all four models. The leader promotes sociability, creates a sense of urgency, stimulates the will to win, and encourages a commitment to shared goals among the team (Sheard & Kakabadse, 2004). Leaders are able to manage opposites, be adaptive to situations, and be context sensitive. Leaders need to consider inclusiveness, innovation, and integrity (Halverson, 1999). Innovation needs freedom, security, and trust. Followers need to sense leaders' willingness. Leaders are responsible for creating adequate environments and cultures for innovations. In the context of the research study, a lack of adequate resources on youth leadership was found. Most references and resources were limited to adult leadership in the context of management and organizations. Most resources related to practices outside Egypt.

Local programs with a focus on youth empowerment and leadership are not present in Egypt (INJAZ, 2010). A number of opportunities are available for which Egyptian youth are eligible, both regionally and internationally. Regionally and through a formal academic program, ALA is a nonprofit organization working to develop and support future generations of African leaders in an attempt to transform Africa. ALA seeks to obtain the 250 most promising young leaders from 54 countries in the developing continent for an innovative 2-year program designed to prepare students for a lifetime of leadership (ALA, 2010). ALA's curriculum focuses on leadership, entrepreneurship, and African studies. Internationally, the Seeds of Peace program prepares future generations for leadership in conflict resolution and peace (Seeds of Peace, 2009). In Chapter 2 under the area of best practices, regional and international programs were documented experiences related to youth leadership development. The programs' listing reflects the deficiency of local youth leadership practices and offerings in Egypt and highlights the importance of the current study as a valuable resource for future youth leadership programming.

Brown Urban (2008) confirmed how current research lacked serious attempts to observe and measure the effective presence of youth development. Innovative approaches are needed to introduce the integration and collaborations between theory-driven research, practitioners, and policymakers in the field of youth programs. The research study, and especially RQ3, contributed to Brown Urban's recommendation and overcame the gap in current knowledge in the area of evaluating youth programs. The literature review section included a description of the lack of evaluation methods and a description of youth leadership and development programs in Egypt and worldwide. RQ3 in the study became an asset to the body of knowledge in the area of youth leadership and development.

Summary

Chapter 2 included the purpose of the literature review and a summary of the title searches, articles, research documents, and journals researched (Creswell, 2005). The chapter started with a germinal framework and a historical overview of the flow and progression of human development theories and current findings about leadership theories. Major learning theories discussed were Vygotsky's proximal development, Dewey's experiential learning, and Bandura's social learning theory. Major discussed leadership theories included trait, transactional, transformational, servant, and others (adaptive, empowering, task-oriented, and women). The sections included the Egyptian context for each topic.

Chapter 2 also included a historical overview and current findings related to the research variables, which were youth leadership competencies, process, and evaluation. The chapter contained an explanation of the definition and development of youth leadership and highlighted the different factors affecting the development of youth leadership. The listed factors included adolescence, education, economic, political, social, religious, and theories (Kress, 2006; Lerner et al., 2005; Ricketts & Rudd, 2002). Literature was related to each factor and then to the Egyptian context (Neuman, 2003). Best practices in Egypt, Africa, the Middle East, and internationally were illustrated. The best practices included both national and organizational practices. The listing also included highlighting the research context under youth leadership competencies, youth leadership process, and youth leadership evaluation in the selected organizational programs. At a later stage of the study, the leadership competencies for youth aged 15–24, the process for youth leadership development, and the effective evaluation tools for youth leadership programs for future programs in Egypt will be identified.

Chapter 3 will contain a description of the purpose of the study, rationale for the research design, discussion of the population and sample, concerns for consent and confidentiality, and processes for data collection and analysis (Maner, 2000; Neuman, 2003). Chapter 3 will include an explanation for selecting the Delphi design, expert panel, and research sample (Maxwell, 2002). Chapter 3 will also include information on how to ensure reliability and validity (de Vaus, 2006; Salkind, 2003).

Chapter 3: Method

The qualitative study supported by quantitative data with a modified Delphi design involved exploring and identifying the needed leadership competencies, processes, and evaluative tools for the development of Egyptian youth leadership programs targeting youth between the ages of 15 and 24. Forty experts and stakeholders in the field of adolescence and leadership development from the greater Cairo metropolitan area in Egypt were identified and invited to participate. The purposively selected experts and stakeholders, who were older than 18 years of age, included educators, parents of young leaders, young leaders (ages 19–24), employers, and community leaders. The geographical location of the study included greater Cairo, which includes the Cairo, Giza, Helwan, Sixth of October, and El Qualubia governorates. All identified experts came from urban locations to ensure their personal and professional exposure to leadership opportunities as participants, professionals, and observers.

Chapter 3 includes a discussion on the rationale for and the appropriateness of selecting the qualitative study supported by quantitative data research method and the Delphi design and on the manner in which the selected research design helped to accomplish the study goals. The chapter also includes a discussion about population, sampling, data collection procedures and rationale, validity, and data analysis. The chapter ends with a summary of the key points presented.

Research Method and Design Appropriateness

A qualitative method supported by quantitative data with a modified Delphi approach was appropriate for collecting data. Both qualitative and quantitative research approaches are similar as they each follow the six-step research process and use the same data collection techniques such as interviews, document review, and observation (Creswell, 2005; de Vaus, 2006; Ruszkiewicz et al., 2006). Qualitative and quantitative research studies differ in the type of problems considered, the handling of literature, research purpose and questions, use and analysis of data, and writing style and structure of the research report (McMillan & Schumacher, 2006).

Quantitative research is an unbiased and objective study that involves asking specific and narrow questions, collecting data, and conducting analysis (Patton, 2002; Simon & Francis, 2004). Researchers set the questions and hypotheses. Quantitative analysis is characterized as standard, has fixed structures and evaluative criteria, and is based on an objective and unbiased approach (Sproull, 2004). The quantitative method includes a technocratic perspective, serves bureaucratic needs, and uses reconstructed logic (Neuman, 2003). Due to the nature of the study, a quantitative method was not applicable to generate the needed results. The study needed a research method that combines reconstructed logic with logic in practice, expert and critical research perspectives, and fixed and cyclical sequencing in the research steps. According to Mills (2003), quantitative research uses measurable and observable data during identifying the purpose of the study. Due to the lack of baseline data about youth leadership in Egypt, the study could not follow the quantitative approach.

A qualitative study includes broad questions to explore the views of the research participants by asking general questions, collecting data that rely on words and text, and analyzing data in a subjective manner (Creswell, 2005; Huberman & Miles, 2002). Taylor, Bogdan, and Walker (2000) suggested that qualitative research is descriptive and directed by the research participants' words, experiences, and observations. Qualitative research is characterized as inductive, naturalistic, holistic, inclusive to different views, flexible, and concerned about meanings related and identified by the research participants (Patton, 2002). Reporting qualitative analysis is subjective, flexible, and has an emerging structure and evaluative criteria (Sproull, 2004).

Qualitative research methods are based on empirical evidence rather than techniques to collect data and are open to change during the research process (Creswell, 2005; Neuman, 2003). Even research questions can change according to the responses of the participants and the flow of the research process (Huberman & Miles, 2002). A qualitative study has major factors to consider when evaluating its scientific merit, which include the persuasive nature of research, the researcher's self-awareness, the audience's needs, and language sensitivity (Cooper & Schindler, 2006). Due to the nature of the research, a qualitative study supported by quantitative data method was more appropriate to explore the needed competencies, process, and evaluation for programs that develop leadership in youth between the ages of 15 and 24 in Egypt.

The mixed method cares for data collected using both qualitative and quantitative research (McMillan & Schumacher, 2006). To understand a research problem, the mixed-methods design is a process for mixing both the quantitative and qualitative data in a single study (Creswell, 2005). Mixed methods contribute to triangulation, a process that helps to provide confirmation of the collected data and to overcome the study's biases (Patton, 2002). Hunt (2007) identified a mixed-method design as the integration of both qualitative and quantitative research through data, techniques, and methods. To ensure the accomplishment of this research's goals, the mixed method was not used.

During the first phase of the research, a qualitative data collection tool was used to assist in exploring the needed youth competencies from five different perspectives: the parental perspectives represented by parents of youth, the educational perspective represented by educators, the perspective of youth represented by youth leaders (ages 19–24), the employment and work perspective represented by employers, and the perspective of society represented by community leaders. During the second phase of the research, a quantitative data was employed through the Delphi controlled feedback and participants' responses to the Likert-type scale questions. As Delphi researchers tend to rely heavily on the qualitative approach, the qualitative study supported by quantitative data method was used in the study as data collection included quantitative data starting with the second round of the Delphi iterations (Iqbal & Pipon-Young, 2009). To explore stakeholders' consensus, the study included a qualitative study supported by quantitative data method with a sequential approach in the use of qualitative and quantitative data.

Research designs include case studies (Creswell, 2005; Yin, 2004), ethnographic design (Patton, 2002; van Maanen, 1998), grounded theory (Glaser & Strauss, 1967), narrative research (Patton, 2002), action research

(Argyris 2000; Creswell, 2005), and Delphi (Leedy & Ormrod, 2001; Linstone & Turoff, 2002; Patton, 2002). In case studies and narrative research, researchers explore individual or organizational stories describing the lives of the research participants (Creswell, 2005). Because the research study was exploratory in nature to define youth leadership competencies, case studies and narrative research methods were limited in offering an appropriate tool to answer the research questions (Bernard, 2005; Marczyk et al., 2005). Researchers and practitioners lack knowledge and local experiences in the field of youth leadership, which does not allow baseline data on the research participants as needed in case studies and narrative research (CEDPA, 2009).

The grounded theory method involves exploring the bonding experiences of research participants to develop a theory (Glaser & Strauss, 1967). Due to the nature of the study, the duration of the study, and the size of the population, choosing the grounded theory method would have led to an unrealistic generalization of developing a theory (Creswell, 2005). Grounded theory was not appropriate for the current study.

Action research is a method for continuous improvement through a cycle of planning, acting, collecting, and reflecting (Mills, 2003). Action research was not possible for implementation in the study due to the exploratory nature of the research. Action research could be used in the future to evaluate the possibility of implementing the findings of the study of youth leadership competencies, processes, and evaluative tools (Creswell, 2005).

For an ethnographic design, the goal for the research study would be to discover the common features of a group of people within a specific culture (Raley, 2005; van Maanen, 1998). Ethnographic designs are qualitative procedures describing, collecting, and documenting stories and experiences of individuals' lives (Creswell, 2005). Genzuk (2003) noted ethnography is a social science research method and can be used in any human arena. Ethnography studies can include "intensive language, culture learning, intensive study of a single field or domain, and a blend of historical, observational, and interview methods" (Genzuk, 2003, p. 1). The research study did not include identifying a specific culture of young leaders, so an ethnographic study would not have been appropriate.

Skulmoski et al. (2007) suggested the Delphi method is needed when researchers need to understand problems, explore opportunities and solutions, or develop forecasts. The research study involved a modified Delphi method to understand the problem of the lack of adequate opportunities for youth leadership development and how to find appropriate solutions for the problem. The Delphi method, which is a qualitative research approach, is an effective method when no reliable past quantitative forecasting is present (Zhao, 2007). Adler and Ziglio (1996) recommended using the Delphi method, which is a tool for knowledge building, when the problem can benefit from a collective subjective judgment.

From among the different research methods and designs, the qualitative study supported by quantitative data method with a modified Delphi design was appropriate, as it was the best fit to ensure the fulfillment of the current research goals and objectives (Custer, Scarcella, & Stewart, 1999). As illustrated in Chapter 2, current literature lacked knowledge and consensus about youth leadership competencies, processes, and evaluative methods. The literature review did not reveal any Delphi studies with the same research problem. The lack of existing Delphi studies on the topic of deficiency in identifying the needed youth leadership competencies, processes, and evaluative tools to build effective leadership programs was an important reason for selecting this method for the study.

A modified Delphi method was the most appropriate method to collect data, ensure consensus in the defined research areas, and ensure adequate answers to the research questions (Cantu, 2003). Researchers use the Delphi method to focus on diverse opinions, values and beliefs before the formation of any action plan, or policy (Brown, 2007). A Delphi technique is future oriented and the aim is to find consensus among experts on future events (Chaw et al., 2001). The study involved obtaining consensus on experts' possible solutions to the identified problem (Hsu & Stanford, 2007a).

Iqbal and Pipon-Young (2009) added that the Delphi method helps researchers to explore a matter that reaches beyond the presently known or believed and contributes to future thinking. The Delphi design is used for both theory and practice (Linstone & Turoff, 2002). Okoli and Pawlowski

(2004) noted the Delphi method contributes to theory building through identifying the variables of interest and generating propositions, generalizing the resulting theory, justifying selected rationale, and contributing to construct validity.

In addition to future prediction, the Delphi method is becoming more popular and effective in the fields of health care, education, and human resources through assessing experts' opinions and consensus, developing policies, and reaching decisions (Clayton, 1997). The Delphi is used in curriculum development and prioritization of outcomes. Franklin and Hart (2006) identified three types of Delphi methods. The three types are classical, decision-making, and policy Delphi. In addition to its different uses, Yousuf (2007) explained how the Delphi method, which can be exploratory, conventional, normative, or fit the policy type, can be used to help put an educational model together. Brown (2007) added that the Delphi method is useful when selected research participants/experts do not necessarily interact to exchange ideas. The Delphi method enables researchers to involve large numbers of geographically and socially different participants (Yousuf, 2007).

Hsu and Sanford (2007a) described the effective use of the Delphi method in specific real-world issues as planning programs, assessing needs, determining policies, using resources, developing alternatives, exploring assumptions, and correlating collective judgment. The Delphi method involves exploring ranges of possible alternatives (Garrod, 2008). Through the Delphi design, all stakeholders actively participated not only in a research study but also by contributing to a lifelong experience that will affect future generations in Egypt.

The Delphi method includes repeated rounds of inquiries, answered by a panel of experts, about possible future developments (Rice, 2009; Stolper et al., 2009; Toth, 1996). The inquiry rounds end with a set of collective conclusions to solve the problem (D. C. Alexander, 2004). To gather expert opinion in a certain field of research, Hennessy and Hicks (2001) suggested using the Delphi method, which is a systematic tiered approach. A Delphi method is the process of using a panel of experts and sequential written questionnaires, controlling anonymous feedback, and reaching an opinion (Patton, 2002).

The use of the Delphi method within leadership studies has been extensive (Campbell, 2007; Huth, 2006; Messinger, 2008; Sheridan, 2005; Whited, 2007). Viehland (2007) commented that the Delphi method is a structured process for eliciting the opinions of a group of experts, reaching a judgment, and validating agreement on an issue related to the future. Yousuf (2007) advised that the basis for deciding on the appropriateness of the Delphi method for a specific research study should be how much the study can benefit from a collective group judgment. The Delphi method can overcome the difficulty of needing a sample to meet face-to-face. Selecting the experts is a vital step in the procedures of the method (Brown, 2007). A clear explanation and description of the study and its purpose need to be introduced to the selected experts to ensure the alignment of their responses to the study objectives (Leedy & Ormrod, 2001). Experts' responses are expected to provide objective information and creative solutions leading to answers to the research problem (Baker et al., 2006). The experts in the current study provided answers regarding how to overcome a deficiency in identifying the needed youth leadership competencies, processes, and evaluative tools to build effective leadership programs.

The participatory approach confirms stakeholders' ownership of research findings and future implementation (Kennedy, 2004). Creswell (2005) referred to the participatory approach as having an impact that contributes to change in our society. Participatory research has special features, such as empowering the study participants based on collaboration in decision making, addressing sensitive issues (such as political, liberation, and democracy), and assisting in self-development and determination (Leedy & Ormrod, 2001). The researcher expected a long-term relationship with the stakeholders for future interest to include implementation.

Using a Delphi method may have advantages and limitations. The Delphi method involves many people over a period of time, which might lead to experts' future commitment and ownership of the implementation process and saves time and rounds of meetings (Slocum, 2005). The Delphi offers anonymity of response, low cost, large sets of data, validity, controlled feedback from the group interaction, and statistical group response (Linstone & Turoff, 2002; Yousuf, 2007). Researchers use the Delphi method when historical data are limited and planning is long.

Researchers need to be aware of the limitations of the method. Based on the number of iterations and the number of included experts, the Delphi method can be time consuming and expensive (Bucknall, 2001). Yousuf (2007) warned researchers to avoid imposing their view onto the sample's opinion and consensus, to avoid overestimating and generalizing the experts' feedback, to avoid using poor summarization and presentation techniques for group responses at the different iterations, and not to ignore disagreements in opinions (Slocum, 2005).

The focus of the modified Delphi study was to identify the needed youth leadership competencies, processes, and evaluative tools to build effective leadership programs. The results of the study may be significant to professionals in the field of youth leadership and development in planning, designing, and evaluating youth leadership programs for youth ages 15–24. Through a modified Delphi method, the study involved investigating the consensus among stakeholders and experts in the field of adolescence and youth leadership development. Consensus was defined a priori to be greater than 80% in the second round (Wenzel, 2008).

Population, Sampling, Data Collection Procedures, and Rationale

To ensure a valid and reliable outcome, Zhao (2007) suggested that a research method should be chosen according to the nature of the problem. According to the nature of the current study, a modified Delphi method was selected to ensure valid and reliable outcomes. Because adequate benchmark information or data on the area to be researched were not available, the Delphi method was the most appropriate method for the current study (Patton, 2002). Slocum (2005) suggested using the Delphi method when the research problem might benefit more from a collective subjective judgment, when the research sample includes multiple backgrounds, when the sample size cannot be accommodated through face-to-face exchange, and when a limitation of resources can hinder frequent group meetings.

Population. Yousuf (2007) described the Delphi method as a group communication and a systematic information gathering process used to resolve a complex problem and project future trends. Through multiple rounds and iterations, the Delphi methodology necessitates a reliance on a panel of experts (D. C. Alexander, 2004; Greenhalgh & Wengraf, 2008; Tsou, 2005). Most Delphi samples consist of an average of 20 participants (Creating Minds, 2008). Zami and Lee (2009) suggested a larger number of experts when using a heterogeneous sample. The target sample size for the current study was 40 experts. For the pilot study, 10 experts, representing the group of stakeholders, received an invitation to participate. The pilot study participants were also invited to nominate other experts to develop the sample through snowball sampling (Miles & Huberman, 1994). The heterogeneous sample included educators, parents, youth (19–24 years old), employers, and community leaders.

According to Skulmoski et al. (2007), panel members or experts are selected based on level of knowledge and experience, availability, and willingness to participate. The sample was chosen using objective and expert-level criteria (Baker et al., 2006; Hargens, 2001). To provide the research study with an exclusive perspective about the researched topic, stakeholder selection should be purposeful and based on the stakeholders' knowledge and willingness to share their insights about the researched topic (Franklin & Hart, 2006).

Jennings et al. (2006) noted youth empowerment and leadership is a social action process with the following levels: personal, family, organizational, and societal. In the current research, selected stakeholders included educators, parents, youth, employers, and community leaders. Many researchers have used the Delphi method with multiple stakeholders (Greenhalgh & Wengraf, 2008; Keil et al., 2002; Macdonald, 2003; Malcolm et al., 2009; Manca et al., 2008; J. Martin, 1991; Masberg et al., 2003; Owens et al., 2008; Rice, 2009; Stolper et al., 2009; Toth, 1996).

Participants who were educators were chosen based on the level of participation (voluntarily or task-based) in the development and implementation of youth leadership activities (e.g., student councils). The sample included educators serving youth ages 15–24. The sample could include teachers, professors, principals, and counselors.

The research participants who were parents had volunteered to serve on leadership-level positions related to the age group 15–24 (e.g., school boards and sports clubs), reared children or youth (15–24 years old), and encouraged their children or youth to join activities with a leadership focus (e.g., Scouts), whether in Egypt or abroad. One parent from each family was welcomed to ensure representation from a diversity of families in the study.

The youth members were emerging adults (ages 19–24). These panel members had participated in a leadership role during their high school years or college in Egypt or abroad (e.g., president of an activity club). This group included students at public or private educational institutions.

The employer stakeholders included representatives from different sectors of employers: nongovernmental organizations, the private sector, the public sector, multinational organizations, and small and medium enterprises. The participants in the employer category were either the owner or the chief executive of an organization that is known to be adopting policies and cultural environments that encourage empowerment and leadership among its entry-level positions (Egyptian International Economic Forum, 2009).

The community leader members were graduates of the Youth Socialism Institute in Egypt from the 1960s. Community leaders held a voluntary leadership position (e.g., board member) in a community-based organization promoting the development and implementation of activities with a focus on youth development and leadership for ages 15–24. Community leaders included religious, political, social, and entrepreneurial representatives. Feedback from community leaders was important to reflect the societal values, cultural customs and traditions, and future leadership needs of communities. Community involvement and continuous assessment are essential elements for educational reform and enhance civil participation and public accountability (Middle East Institute, 2008).

To accelerate the process of data collection and to accommodate the experts' busy schedules, data collection was conducted using Web-based questionnaires (Masberg et al., 2003). The panel was handled as an aggregate group for all response data except for the initial affiliation identification and first-round iteration results. The selected panel's personal demographic records were not traced or associated with responses after the first round.

Heterogeneity of the participants ensures the validity of the results (Slocum, 2005). Okoli and Pawlowski (2004) noted heterogeneous groups are more creative than homogeneous groups in decision making. The focus of the current research study was on the heterogeneity of the selected sample. Through three different rounds of Web-based questionnaires, the domination of certain characters in the sample, whether by quantity or personality strength, was eliminated (Manca et al., 2008).

Sampling. Through the sampling process, researchers study and select units from the chosen population to generalize the results back to the population (Trochim, 2006). Larson and Farber (2003) classified research samples into probability and nonprobability samples. According to Vogt (2007), random probability sampling includes stratified (all segments of the population), cluster (natural subgroups), and systematic (ordered numerically).

Champion (2006) described the nonprobability sampling technique as selecting elements based on accessibility. Neuman (2003) noted qualitative research methods can use one of seven types of nonprobability or nonrandom sampling: "haphazard, quota, purposive, snowball, deviant case, sequential, and theoretical" (p. 211). Purposive sampling is associated with qualitative research (Palys, 2008). For exploratory research, Galloway (2005) suggested using a nonprobability sample.

According to Ervin (2002), nonprobability sampling includes convenience, quota, random assignment to groups, and purposive sampling. Aaker, Kumar, and Day (2007) described nonprobability sampling as judgmental (expert-based), convenience (convenient units), quota (use of subgroups), and snowball (small and specialized). Nonprobability sampling includes convenience and purposive sampling (Trochim, 2006). Purposive sampling includes modal instance, expert, quota, diversity, and snowball.

Palys (2008) added purposive sampling includes stakeholder, deviant case, typical case, paradigmatic case, maximum variation, criterion, theory-guided, critical case, disconfirming, and expert sampling.

The sample in the current study used a snowball Delphi panel including stakeholders from across the life spectrum of a young leader, including educators, parents, youth (19–24 years), employers, and community leaders. Heckathorn (2002) noted snowball sampling starts with a set of initial participants who serve as seeds for an increasing chain of referrals. Masberg et al. (2003) referred to snowball sampling as network sampling. The study included snowball nonprobability sampling with exploratory research to select the participants to fulfill the research purpose. Wright and Stein (2005) defined snowball sampling as a chain referral method. In snowball sampling, a sample is formed from a base of primary contacts, which are requested to communicate the introduction and refer their associates. Recognized experts or leaders received an invitation to participate in the pilot study and started the nomination process of experts.

A snowball sample builds up in size as the primary contacts suggest the names and/or addresses of others, who fulfill specific criteria (Galloway (2005). As the nomination process starts, nominating experts were advised clearly about the selection criteria for each identified stakeholder category, which was educators, parents, youth (19–24 years), employers, and community leaders. The data collection process started after the sample size reached 40 and after nominated participants signed the informed consent. To ensure the inclusion of the female perspective, gender equality, and participation diversity, the study sample targeted more than 50% female participation (Babbie, 2007).

Maxwell (2002) warned researchers of systematic generalizations to wider populations without careful consideration of the researched context and overall population. Generalization can either be internal or external. Generalization is the process of generalizing studied results in certain community, group, or institution to others that were not directly observed or interviewed (Maxwell, 2002). Under a purposive nonprobability sample, researchers should consider the special nature and characteristics of the account (setting or population) observed before stepping into external generalization (Schofield, 2002). Due to the expert level of the selected recognized experts in the pilot study, nominated participants in the actual research study, and classification of the stakeholders in this research study, external generalization was not possible.

Informed consent. Through the informed consent form (see Appendix A), the participants learned about the study's intent, significance, and procedures. The informed consent started with an introductory letter that welcomed the participants, explained the purpose of the research study, and listed terms and conditions associated with the consent. The consent indicated that no potential risk to participating existed beyond that of daily life. All participants were asked to sign the consent for approval to use their responses in the research study and to indicate their full understanding of the research study duration and design.

After receiving approval from the University of Phoenix Academic Review Board, the selection process of the study participants began. Through extensive work in youth development and professional networks, the researcher contacted 10 recognized experts representing the stakeholder groups of the study (educators, parents, youth leaders, employers, and community leaders). The recognized experts were credible and respectable, primary stakeholders in the study area, and ready to support the study by nominating potential panelists (Hsu & Sanford, 2007b). To overcome possible biases, each recognized expert was expected to nominate potential panelists for each stakeholder category with different opinions about the research topic and different social backgrounds (Routi, 2007). Each recognized expert was expected to nominate at least 10 participants. The larger pool of potential panelists provided stand-by participants to cover any withdrawals before or during the first round of the study.

The researcher contacted the nominated lists of panelists through e-mail (Masberg et al., 2003). The initial contact involved an attempt to establish a direct and open line of communication, explain the focus and necessity of the study, present participation criteria, introduce the nomination process, respond to questions, and verify potential participants' interest in participating in the study. During the initial contact, the researcher was able to discover interest and availability. Nomination and recruitment continued until the required number of sample participants was reached (Wright & Stein, 2005). The study was fully designed and conducted in English. In case of lack of interest, the researcher would have invited potential participants to nominate others.

Upon expression of interest to participate in the study, the researcher asked the participant to complete the consent form and return it within 1 week by e-mail. Participants were contacted at least 1 week before the study start date to ensure participants' commitment and completion of the informed consent. The informed consent contained a complete section on withdrawal procedures in case of no availability or lack of interest. Participants could have withdrawn at any time from the study with no penalty. The withdrawal process was to contact the researcher in a written format, state the reason for withdrawal, and suggest another expert who might be interested in joining the study. After Round 1, participants could withdraw following the same procedures but the participants would not be requested to nominate other experts.

The informed consent also contained the researcher's full contact information. Nominated participants were invited to pose clarifying questions regarding the informed consent and research study. If participants had any concerns during or following the study, they were encouraged to contact the researcher in writing and list their questions. During the study, a concerned participant would receive a written response within 24 hours. Following the study, the researcher would respond to the concerned participant within 5 working days of receiving the concern or question. Upon approval of the study and its publication by ProQuest, the researcher plans to send a notification and a copy of the research to all participants involved in the study.

The researcher also plans to keep all collected data for a 3-year period following the completion of the study in case any questions or concerns arise. Upon the completion of the 3-year period, the hard copies of any collected data will be shredded and any soft copies will be reformatted. During the study, the computer carrying the collected data had a restricted password and was placed in a safe location. To ensure the privacy and protection of the participants' data, the room in which the computer and hard copies of the data were stored at the researcher's home was securely locked. The researcher was the only person accessing the e-mails and responses from the research participants. Hsu and Sanford (2007b) suggested offering the Delphi panelists financial or material incentives, but due to cultural sensitivity to offering financial incentives, no incentives were offered.

Ethical nature of the study. The two major ethical concerns existed in the scientific facts and the participants' rights. Researchers must guarantee the privacy, confidentiality, and anonymity of the studied sample (Wenzel, 2008). In relation to the data, researchers need to relate details of the study design with the results and relate results with the collected data (Neuman, 2003). Mack et al. (2009) referred to the universal basis for research ethics as respect for persons, beneficence, justice, and respect for communities. To ensure respect, the seed questions for the pilot study were based on the literature review. The pilot study was intended to test the questions of Round 1 and the reliability of the data collection instrument used. To ensure respect for individuals, the researcher was considerate to the dignity of participants when inviting participants to join the study, drafting the questionnaire, communicating controlled feedback, and disseminating research results (Johnson & Christensen, 2002). Informed consent was another tool to stress the concept of respect for individuals. The researcher treated participants as partners and stakeholders rather than as a means to reach objectives of the study. To ensure beneficence, the researcher articulated through the informed consent form that research participants would not face any risks and could benefit from participating in the study. Participants were also advised that there would be no penalties associated with withdrawing from the study. To ensure justice, the researcher planned to disseminate research results to all research participants. To ensure the respect of communities, the researcher considered the values and traditions of the Egyptian culture.

Data collection procedures. Salkind (2003), Mills (2003), and Mack et al. (2009) explained various data collection techniques for qualitative research, including interviews, documentation, focus groups, archival records, observation, and physical artifacts. In an exploratory research study, survey data collection would be suitable (Neuman, 2003). The modified Delphi study included questionnaires as the main instrument for data collection over three rounds of circulation among five stakeholder groups. To ensure consensus in a Delphi study, Iqbal and Pipon-Young (2009) suggested that researchers conduct three or more rounds. A pilot test of the questions of the first round of the Delphi tiers took place. The pilot study included 10 participants with an equal distribution of two participants from each of the five population stakeholder groups in the study. The pilot group was introduced to the process of data collection through the first-round questionnaire. The pilot group members were experts and leaders who started the nomination process of the research participants. Based on the feedback of the pilot group, the questionnaire was modified before the data collection process began. Data analysis took place continuously through the three rounds of the modified Delphi method.

At the end of each round, the results among the different stakeholders were summarized, listed, and included in the following round of the questionnaire process. Adler and Ziglio (1996) noted how a Delphi process should supply experts with other experts' thinking, assessment and forecast assumptions. As the three questionnaires were Web-based, all participants were anonymous to each other. The researcher facilitated the group communication, collected the answers, summarized responses, and shared results with all stakeholders. Results were classified per stakeholder but shared anonymously with all participants.

The questionnaires were Web-based and conducted through SurveyMonkey (2008), a free Internet-based data collection tool. Following the registration, each participant received a short welcome e-mail. According to SurveyMonkey's privacy policy, the website would not use the collected information in any way. The researcher's information and collected data were secured in the strictest confidence and environment.

To start the data collection process, an e-mail was sent to invite all research participants to join the study. The invitation included a clear description of the study, time frame, expected role of participants, and informed consent form. Participants could respond within 2 weeks and submit any inquiries about the study. After collecting all consent forms and conducting the pilot study, the first questionnaire was launched. Each of the three Delphi rounds was expected to last approximately for 1-3 months, including analysis, controlled feedback, and drafting the following round. To create group consensus regarding the necessary competencies, processes, and evaluative tools for effective leadership programs for youth (ages 15–24) in Egypt, selected experts participated in the modified Delphi study through interacting with the researcher and anonymously with the group of experts.

After the pilot study, Round 1 started and participants were asked to respond to the open-ended questions in a narrative format. The questions were set to serve the study's purpose and objectives and to encourage participants to give detailed qualitative responses. Upon the analysis of the experts' responses, participants received aggregate data for revision and feedback, which was used in the development of questions for the second round.

The research study included the use of a modified Delphi technique to seek consensus. As the study involved a search for agreement, Round 2 included a 5-point rating scale matching responses to *very important, important, neutral, not very important,* and *not important.* In the third round, experts received their comments from the second round with a mean equal or higher than 4.0 for each theme and subtheme. To ensure consensus, experts were requested to reorder statements based on the mean responses and feedback from the other experts. Participants were encouraged to give any necessary comments. After participants completed the third questionnaire, a thank-you message was sent (see Appendix K).

Types of data. In social research, qualitative studies adopt a nonlinear, transcendent, and logic application in real-life situations (Neuman, 2003). In the first Delphi round, the research should include soft data that are in the form of thoughts, words or statements, and photos or symbols (Neuman, 2003). In the research study, the collected data were based on the experts' words, sentences, and recommendations toward youth leadership competencies, processes, and evaluative tools. The current research study followed a cyclic approach in obtaining experts' input and feeding the data into the cycle of progressing toward answering and refining the answers of the research questions during the three Delphi rounds (Garrod, 2008). The research study involved an attempt to move from divergent to convergent consensus of the experts' feedback (Hsu & Stanford, 2007a).

In the first round, the researcher used open-ended questions to generate data (Zami & Lee, 2009). Open-ended questions have the ability to induce responses that are meaningful and culturally related, unexpected by the researcher and rich and descriptive in nature (Creswell, 2005). Through the first Delphi round, Iqbal and Pipon-Young (2009) commented that the study's reliability and validity may be enhanced if research experts produce the items. Starting Round 2, participants were asked to rank according to importance their responses generated in Round 1 through a 5-point Likert-type scale (Masberg et al., 2003).

Instrument reliability. Researchers should consider the elimination of bias during the process of data collection. Steinberg (2004) noted researchers' awareness of personal bias is the most crucial step in handling qualitative research. Researcher bias can range from directing participants toward a specific topic to hiding evidence in the analysis stage. To ensure bias elimination, researchers need to consciously and explicitly think about bias, obtain feedback on interpretations from others, use different ways of coding, and stay open to change (Neuman, 2003; Zami & Lee, 2009). The researcher was expected to be honest and professional about considering all data, including any participants' disagreements. To eliminate possible biases, the researcher was flexible to accommodating changes in the development of the questionnaires at each round.

Steinberg (2004) noted that researchers need to consider the intended audience, develop implications for the audience, and speak clearly to them; consider transferability (be clear about where and when findings can apply); use a variety of evidence; present findings in an exhaustive way; and use active self-reflection to limit personal biases. In the current research study, reliability was targeted through clear explanation (e.g., research's intent, terms, duration), instructions for completing the Web-based questionnaires, and limiting the acceptance of new participants before the start of the second Delphi round.

Hargens (2001) noted errors in human populations can affect the accuracy of surveys. Errors in human population can be related to non response rate, interviewing errors, and measurement errors. In the current research study, participants engaged in controlled feedback to prevent data collection errors. To reduce no response errors, the researcher sent regular reminders to the participants and explained how their feedback was essential to the validity of the study (Hsu & Stanford, 2007b). Reminder messages were sent after 1 week of launching the questionnaires across the three rounds.

Proper seed questions could contribute positively to the reliability of the study (Zami & Lee, 2009). The pilot study included the use of seed questions. The seed questions were as follows:

1. In your pre-university leadership opportunities, what skills and competencies did you possess that were most helpful (please list all that apply)?

2. During your university/adult leadership opportunities, what skills and competencies did you possess that were most helpful (please list all that apply)?

3. In your experience, what leadership competencies in other people have you observed to be the most important to develop (please list all that apply)?

4. In your opinion, in what ways or in which type of opportunities can youth (ages 15–24) be taught leadership competencies?

5. In your opinion, how can leadership opportunities and programs for youth (ages 15–24) be effectively evaluated?

6. In your opinion, what other additional information related to youth leadership was not covered in the questionnaire?

All the seed questions were crafted to uncover expert opinion on the youth leadership competencies, processes, and evaluative tools needed to build effective leadership programs in the future. The seed questions were also associated to the theoretical framework, which was based on the developmental contextualization (Lerner et al., 2005). Data obtained from the literature review were used to draft exploratory questions. The questions were broad and open-ended to ensure a range of narrative responses. Responses from the first round were analyzed for themes and patterns to be the foundation for designing a 5-point Likert-type importance scale that includes the following choices: *very important, important, neutral, not very important,* and *not important.* In Round 3, participants were supplied with responses from the second round with the mean response value for identified statements. To reach final consensuses, participants were able to reconsider ranking the statements in accordance to the mean responses and narrative feedback from the other participants.

Validity and Reliability

To maintain data integrity, researchers must consider validity and reliability of the data collected and ethical issues in research. In designing and analyzing quality qualitative research studies, validity and reliability should be considered (Patton, 2002). Although concepts of validity and reliability are correlated to quantitative studies, Healy and Perry (2000) confirmed that each research paradigm has its own terms and judging criterion. In qualitative research, Golafshani (2003) conceptualized validity and reliability as trustworthiness, rigor, and quality. As essential criteria for quality research, Lincoln & Guba (1985) suggested the use of credibility, confirmability, dependability, and transferability in qualitative studies. Research validity refers to the truthfulness of proposal, inferences, or conclusions (Neuman, 2003). Validity refers to the realization of the researcher's concept through the measures used (Patton, 2002). In the following section, validity and reliability will be discussed through suggested validity concepts of Lincoln & Guba (1985).

To ensure the validity concept of credibility, trustworthiness of the study should be addressed. Credibility is related to the truefulness inferences concerning cause-effect relationships (Trochim, 2006). Because the current research was exploratory, high credibility could be achieved (Howell, 2005). Credibility relates to controlling errors in the research design (Neuman, 2003). If the principles of qualitative research are pursued, the analysis quality will be ensured (Morse et al., 2002). The Academic Review Board process and scholar committees helped to eliminate design errors. Creswell (2005) reported that credibility can be achieved through triangulation, expert selection and review, and a participatory approach to research.

First, triangulation is a validity procedure seeking convergence among multiple methods or sources of data to develop common themes and categories in a research study (Creswell & Miller, 2000). According to Neuman (2003), triangulation is the process of studying the research from different angles and perspectives. Triangulation can include theoretical, data, methodological, investigator, multiple, and analysis triangulation. Triangulation of theory, which is the use of various theories in research planning and result interpretation, was used (Creswell, 2005). Because the research design involved a modified Delphi method, the questionnaire was the only data collection tool used. Triangulation was reached through the three rounds of the Delphi study and participants' review of their responses through the controlled feedback process. To provide quantitative data, Round 2 included closed-ended questions with a Likert-type scale to select predetermined themes and statements on a 5-point scale of importance. Through the three rounds, the questions item sequence for both the open-ended and closed-ended questions was the same. Because a group consensus was necessary, the modified Delphi technique included both qualitative and quantitative data and triangulation was achieved.

Second, expert selection and review process need to follow a set criteria and systematic procedure. Researchers need to focus on choosing appropriate experts and appropriate stakeholders to ensure validity of the design (Okoli & Pawlowski, 2004). The researcher ensured that nominations followed the set criteria for each stakeholder group (Syed et al., 2009). Upon receiving all nominations, the researcher divided nominated participants into the five stakeholder groups according to their qualifications and fit to the set criteria. Each participant was only listed in one identified stakeholder group. The list of nominees was ranked in priority for invitation to join the study. After the sample size was reached, the invitation process stopped and Round 1 started. Additional nominations were saved in case of any withdrawals that might have taken place before Round 2.

Third, a participatory approach to research supports credibility. In the current study, the accuracy of qualitative findings was ensured through continuous feedback from the experts about approving their earlier responses. Responses were provided anonymously and in an aggregate manner. The study was participatory, as selected experts were involved in all research phases. After each round of surveying, participants should review their earlier responses to validate the researcher's interpretation (Okoli & Pawlowski, 2004). The research process included the use of reality maps to facilitate the emergence of collective intelligence and the process of expert consensus. Skulmoski et al. (2007) described reality maps as graphical representation of main constructs under study. Reality maps represent reality from the participants' perspective and highlight "interaction, causes and effects, process flow, and other aspects of their reality" (Skulmoski et al., 2007, p. 2). Starting in the second round, the research included a reality map illustrating a summary of the previous round in a graphical illustration to improve participants' understanding.

To ensure the validity concept of transferability, generalization of the research results should be addressed (de Vaus, 2006; Salkind, 2003). In the current study, high transferability was not possible to obtain because of the explicit nature and background of the sample and its geographic location as described in Chapter 1. Schofield (2002) explained that transferability can be irrelevant due to cultural anthropology (e.g., population, situation, time, design). In the current study, the modified Delphi sample was appropriate in the number of experts participating in the study (Cantu, 2003) but the sample's opinion was not adequate to represent the entire population in Egypt and other regions. Maxwell (2002) noted qualitative research is inductive and cares for understanding the sample rather than generalizing the research results. Unrepresentative samples might limit the ability to generalize research (de Vaus, 2006). To overcome the unrepresentative sample, future research will be carried out to generalize the findings for Egypt and the MENA region as discussed in Chapter 5.

To ensure the validity concept of confirmability, research objectivity through documenting the data collection and analysis procedures should be discussed (Trochim, 2006). The researcher explained and documented Delphi expert selection, data collection, and analysis procedures. In addition to achieving confirmability, transferability can be achieved through comprehensive and detailed descriptions (Wenzel, 2008). To ensure transparency and validity in the study, discrepant responses contradicting the recognized themes were included. Participants' responses and recommendations about the research process were included.

To ensure the validity concept of dependability, consistency or reliability is addressed. In qualitative research methods, researchers are responsible for the reliability of knowledge produced by study, moral, and professional obligation for an ethical study. Researcher's responsibility and examination of consistency should include both the process and product of the research (Hoepfl, 1997). Reliability is a consequence of the validity in a study (Patton, 2002).

To ensure reliability, Adler and Ziglio (1996) suggested that researchers test the iteration questionnaires and feedback given, guarantee structured group communication, apply the experts' criteria, and provide key words and clear instructions to the experts in answering the questionnaires. The seed questions written for the pilot study and Delphi Round 1 were based on findings from the literature review in Chapter 2. The study included a pilot study among 10 recognized experts to test the first questionnaire for Delphi Round 1 and controlled feedback. The pilot study aided in reaching content validity and reliability of the data collection instrument. Later in the study, the participants were able to revise their responses through the controlled feedback after each round of the Delphi (Okoli & Pawlowski, 2004). The Web-based questionnaires included clear instructions on how to find the questionnaires online, fill in the answers, and submit the completed questionnaires.

Because the research study involved questionnaires as the main tool for data collection, the instrument's validity and reliability needed to be evaluated. According to the International Development Research Center (2009), researchers using questionnaires need to avoid closed questions, open questions without proper guidelines, unclear or leading questions, and an illogical order of questions. In drafting all three rounds of questionnaires, the suggestions made by the International Development Research Center were followed. In the pilot study and Round 1, the seed questions had an exploratory nature (Shank, 2006). Guidelines for each questionnaire were carefully drafted to avoid misleading the study participants.

Participants had 2 weeks to respond to the questionnaire in each round. Reminders to non-respondents occurred through e-mail or via a telephone call (Hsu & Sanford, 2007b). To reduce non-respondent rates, Aaker et al. (2007) suggested re-contacting the non-respondents through a callback system. Callback systems may include regular reminders up to six times. Reminder messages were used for non-respondents. At the end of Round 3, all participants received a thank-you note expressing appreciation for stakeholders' responses and participation. After the completion of the research, the conclusion of the study would be shared with the participants and recognized leaders and experts.

To give a true assessment of time commitment, participants were advised that each questionnaire in the three rounds would take a maximum of 15 minutes with a total of 45 minutes over the duration of 3 to 9 months. Upon receiving the participants' signed informed consents, the researcher sent an invitation through e-mail to start the Round 1 questionnaire. The e-mail message included clear instructions about the questionnaire and a hyperlink to the questionnaire.

To ensure rigor research, qualitative studies rely on the investigator's responsiveness and verification strategies (Morse et al., 2002). To attain optimal validity and reliability, research investigator needs to be open, sensitive, and creative in tendering any ideas that research results do not support. Verification strategies include methodological coherence, sampling appropriateness, collecting and analyzing data concurrently, thinking theoretically, and theory development (Morse et al., 2002). In the current qualitative study, the researcher was flexible and considered all ideas and feedback provided by the participants through the pilot study and Delphi iterations. The researcher implemented all verification strategies except for the theory development. Methodological coherence, sampling appropriateness, and collecting and analyzing data concurrently are explained in Chapter 1, 3, and 4. The thinking theoretically strategy is provided through Chapter 2 and 5.

Data Analysis

According to Neuman (2003), data comprise the empirical evidence or information that researchers gather carefully following rules and procedures. Data can take a numerical or nonnumerical format. Researchers are always considering several means to manage their raw data to answer their research questions in qualitative studies and to formalize their hypotheses in quantitative research for a conclusion of acceptance or refusal. Data handling includes data access, storage, and retrieval (Shank, 2006). Researchers try to find suitable ways to transform pieces of data for computer input and use tables and figures to present and summarize, interpret, and relate results to theories. After collecting data, researchers analyze and interpret the data. Researchers also write a research report to inform others about the study's background, design and procedures, and findings. The current study included the use of qualitative and quantitative analysis to find relationships and agreements among each stakeholder and across the five stakeholder groups (Skulmoski et al., 2007). At the end of first iterations, the collected data were classified based on the responses from each stakeholder and on the relationships between responses and identified demographics (e.g., male, female, age; Macdonald, 2003; Toth, 1996).

According to Salkind (2003), a coding system is the process of transferring data from the collected format to a data analysis format. A coding system needs to be clear and unambiguous to prevent losing the meaning of the data. Data need to be recorded as explicit and discrete. A coding system was used to code and decode the collected data.

Coding is the means researchers use to reorganize data and transform the data from one form to another for analysis purposes (Neuman, 2003). Researchers usually code data to transform them to a new format that can be easily processed using a computer. Data analysis refers to the way in which researchers are able to manage data and retrieve relevant parts (De Vaus,

2006). Data analysis includes the examination, sorting, categorization, evaluation, comparison, synthesis, and contemplation of coded data (Denzin, 2002). Data analysis also involves reviewing and recording raw data. Coding is an integral vital part of the data analysis process (Huberman & Miles, 2002).

According to Neuman (2003), data analysis is a central part of the research process. Data analysis helps to conclude inference and a judgment based on empirical data. Qualitative data analysis has several strategies, which are "the narrative, ideal types, successive approximation, the illustrative method, path dependency and contingency, domain analysis, and analytic comparison" (Neuman, 2003, p. 447). In the current research, the illustrative method was the most suitable strategy for data analysis. The illustrative method is the process of complementing theory with qualitative data (Barber & Korbanka, 2003).

The Web-based commercial survey, SurveyMonkey, was used for the data collection process. Upon acquiring completed responses from the 40 participants, the data analysis started. Responses were downloaded to a PDF file format to analyze responses inductively and categorize them into common themes. Identified emergent themes were used later in the development of Round 2 survey items. The data were coded and classified according to participants' code and stakeholders' category. Responses were examined and organized for commonalities in ideas, themes, and patterns.

Using the affinity diagram, responses were reviewed and analyzed qualitatively to find the common themes and illustrate results in a graphical representation. The affinity diagram ensures an orderly process for reviewing information and representing ideas in a visual manner to form categories. The affinity diagram was used to compile information and organize it into natural classifications (Haselden & Algozzine, 2003).

To ensure a logical and consistent base for the theme-based categories developed, the study included an inductive analysis technique to explore the qualitative data collected in Round 1. The data analysis included manual counting and recounting the information provided by the participants, compressing data, summarizing and exploring patterns, and validating identified themes. Simple methods were used for the collected data and research problem (Wilkinson, 1999). The use of spreadsheets and interpretation techniques helped to find theme frequencies and classifications with limited rewording to ensure consistency in themes and meaning. Themes were also classified according to research questions.

The research involved attempts through data analysis to reduce large amounts of narrative information and find patterns and relationships among the categories and collected data. The collected data were categorized based on themes, concepts, and similar features, according to the research questions (Neuman, 2003). Because of the ease involved with open coding, data were classified under RQ1, RQ2, and RQ3, which are labels for the three research questions. In addition, further coding was used for the different stakeholders: educators (EDU), parents (P), youth (Y), employers (E), and community leaders (CL). The researcher used other letter codes for the context of the research questions: competencies (LC), processes (LP), and evaluation tools (LE). The researcher used numbers accordingly to express sequence.

Neuman (2003) identified open coding as the first attempt to abridge collected data into major categories. The data were then classified under themes according to a second iteration of analysis through axial coding. Because the design of the current research was a Delphi method, the responses of the experts were not anticipated, and the themes could not be determined before collecting data. At the end of the data analysis, selective coding was used, which included all scanned data and preceding codes. By merging abstract concepts with the collected empirical data, new concepts were generated. Researchers need to use both the descriptive statistics and the inferential statistics in the data analysis process (Salkind, 2003).

For data interpretation, Denzin (2002) explained the six steps of the interpretive process: framing research questions, deconstructing, capturing, bracketing, constructing, and contextualizing phenomena. The researcher followed the suggested six steps. During the current modified Delphi study, a pilot study was conducted using 10 recognized experts who represented equally the five stakeholder groups of educators, parents, youth (19–24 years), employers, and community leaders. The pilot study participants responded to the seed questions included in the Instrument Reliability section of this chapter.

In each round of the questionnaires, data was gathered from the participants on an individual basis. Through controlled feedback, participants were able to communicate to the researcher their judgment for each round. Feedback from the pilot study affected the formation of seed questions in the first round. Questions in Round 1 were open-ended, connecting to the research questions. Participants were advised to respond individually and in a narrative format. In Round 2, statements were crafted thematically from the narrative responses of the experts in the first round.

Summary

The focus of Chapter 3 was the rationale of the chosen research approach and design. The current research study included a qualitative-method approach supported by quantitative data with a modified Delphi research design. The study included both qualitative and quantitative data (Bernard, 2000). In the first round, the research used qualitative data. Myers (2000) noted qualitative research is dedicated to explore meaning and understanding and not to predict outcomes or verify truth. Starting with the second round, the research used quantitative data.

To identify themes, responses of the first Delphi round were processed qualitatively. The study included the use of identified themes to create a set of questions for the questionnaire in the second round. Participating experts were requested to rate identified themes and subthemes on a Likert-type scale. In the third round, mean results of Round 2 responses were provided. Participants had the opportunity to modify their responses based on the collective data provided.

Salkind (2003) identified the research design as the researcher's choice of available methods and structures of an investigation to perform data collection and analysis. The modified Delphi design fit the research problem. The selected research design was the design most able to fulfill the enquiry gaps of the research questions.

Chapter 3 included an illustration of the research method and design appropriateness, population, sampling, and data collection procedures and rationale. The current research included the snowball sampling process (Patton, 2002). The sample included a Delphi panel with 40 experts. The sample included five stakeholder groups: educators, parents, youth (19–24 years), employers, and community leaders. Rice (2009) noted snowball sampling is suitable to identify participants with unique characteristics who are able to nominate others.

Chapter 3 also included issues related to validity, reliability, and data analysis. Shank (2006) referred to the trustworthiness approach in overcoming qualitative research difficulties in acquiring reliability, validity, and generalizability. The trustworthiness approach includes dependability, credibility, transferability, and conformability of the research results (Lincoln & Guba, 1985). Chapter 3 also contained a description of the sources of data, the data analysis, and the ethical nature of the current study (Neuman, 2003). Chapter 3 included an explanation of the expert selection process, informed consent, and method of communication with the Delphi experts. Chapter 4 will contain a discussion of the data analysis, findings, and results of the study.

Chapter 4: Analysis and Results

The purpose of the qualitative study supported by quantitative data with a modified Delphi design was to explore, examine, and refine the leadership skills and competencies needed for young Egyptian leaders to determine how to develop multiple youth development and leadership opportunities for youth at ages 15–24 and to establish necessary effective evaluative methods. Leadership competencies that need incorporating in successful youth leadership programs were the unit for the study. The geographic location of the study covered the greater Cairo zone, which includes Cairo, Giza, Helwan, Sixth of October, and El Qualubia governorates.

This chapter contains the results, analyses, and findings of the Delphi iteration of responses of the five stakeholder groups: educators, parents, youth (ages 19–24), employers, and community leaders. The sample included 40 identified experts to participate in a three-round survey to gain consensus on the competencies needed to develop appropriate and effective youth leadership programs for youth between the ages of 15 and 24. In this chapter, results are illustrated according to the Delphi iterations and Research Questions.

As available literature did not include knowledge and consensus about youth leadership competencies, processes, and evaluative methods, a modified Delphi design was selected to ensure the fulfillment of the goals and objectives of the research. Chapter 3 explained the rationale for using a modified Delphi method to obtain group agreement (Linstone & Turoff, 2002) and described the data collection process through a three-round survey, including open-ended questions, Likert-type scaling, and ranking of expert results. The three-round method was presented to the nominated participants through the online questionnaire instrument SurveyMonkey.

Responses from the first round were analyzed for themes and patterns to be used as the foundation for designing a 5-point Likert-type scale in Round 2. The scale included the following choices: *very important, important, neutral, not very important,* and *not important.* In Round 3, participants were requested to give feedback and agreement about the data provided in Round 2. Consensus for each question was determined when 80% or more of the panelists were in agreement, which is represented by a weighted mean rating equivalent to or higher than a rating of 4.0. To reach final consensus, participants were asked to rank the statements in accordance to the mean responses and narrative feedback from the other participants.

Sample Demographics

For the pilot study, the first round questionnaire was sent to 10 recognized experts representing the five stakeholder groups. Eight recognized experts responded to the pilot study. Two participants were 19–28 years old, three participants were 29–38 years old, one was 39–48 years old, and two were 49–58 years old. No pilot participants were older than 58. Five participants were females and three were males. Three pilot participants were from Cairo, two from Giza, one from Helwan, one from Sixth of October, and one from El Qualubia. Five pilot participants were college educated; three had masters of arts degrees or masters of sciences degrees. One participant was listed under others, listing "the attainment of early childhood diploma." The stakeholder classifications were one parent, three educators, one youth (19–24), one employer, and two community leaders. Two participants chose two stakeholder classifications.

Participants in Round 1 fulfilled the sample specifications of eight participants per stakeholder group: educators, parents, youth (age 19–24), employers, and community leaders. The sample covered the greater Cairo zone, which included Cairo, Giza, Helwan, Sixth of October, and El Qualubia governorates. The sample also contained a higher percentage of female than male participation, with a total of 55% as demonstrated in Table 2.

Table   2

Participants' Gender

Answer options	%	n
Female	55.0	22
Male	45.0	18

The highest percentage of age group participation was for the category of 19–28 years, with 32.5% of participants. Participants who age 49 years old and older represented 17.5%. No responses were recorded for the category of others (see Table 3).

Table 3

Participants' Age

Answer options	%	n
19–28	32.5	13
29–38	27.5	11
39–48	22.5	9
49–58	12.5	5
Older	5.0	2
Other (please specify)		0

All research participants were expected to have a college education. Eighteen participants (45.0%) were recorded as having a bachelor's degree. Participants with graduate-level education (MA, MS, or doctoral degrees) comprised 55.0% of the population (see Table 4). No participants selected the others category.

Table 4

Participants' Education

Answer options	%	n
Bachelor degree	45.0	18
Master's degree	42.5	17
Doctoral degree	12.5	5
Others	0.0	0
Other (please specify)		0

Data Collection and Analysis Procedures

To create group consensus regarding the necessary competencies, processes, and evaluative tools for effective leadership programs for youth (ages 15–24) in Egypt, selected experts participated in the modified Delphi study by interacting with the researcher and anonymously with the group of experts. The three Delphi rounds lasted for 9 months (April 2011 to December 2011) and included analysis, controlled feedback, and drafting the following rounds. The three Delphi rounds included open-ended questions, Likert-type scale, and ranking of identified themes. Prior to the three Delphi rounds and the formal data collection process, a pilot study was conducted.

Pilot study. The pilot study included the five stakeholder groups in the study. The pilot group was introduced to the process of data collection through the first-round questionnaire. The pilot group consisted of recognized experts and leaders who started the nomination process of the research participants. Based on the feedback of the pilot group, the questionnaire was modified as needed before the data collection process began.

To ensure an adequate response rate at the pilot study, the first questionnaire was sent to 10 recognized experts, consisting of two experts per stakeholder group (see Appendix B). Eight experts responded, completed the questionnaire, and signed the informed consent (see Appendix A). All eight participants nominated other research participants and supplied e-mail addresses. No reminders were sent as the pilot group responded promptly.

Two participants commented, "The questionnaire was clear" and "easy to complete." One participant suggested breaking the instructions into bullet points for clarity. In the first round of the actual study, the instructions for the leadership experience were modified and listed as bullet points. Another suggestion was to change the fourth seed question, which was "In your opinion, in what ways, or in which types of opportunities, can youth (ages 15–24) be taught leadership competencies?" to "In your opinion, in what ways can youth (ages 15–24) be taught leadership competencies? Which types of opportunities can youth be provided?" No similar suggestions or comments were received. The pilot responses for the mentioned question did not reflect any misunderstanding to the content or purpose of the question. The suggested modification for the fourth seed question was not implemented in the first round of the actual study.

In the pilot study, the questionnaire was sent to all stakeholders through one e-mail message explaining the purpose of the study, attaching the consent form to the original message, and including the hyperlink for the questionnaire. In the first round, the nominated participants were contacted through e-mail messages based on their stakeholder classification. The fifth question under demographic data, which specifies the type of stakeholder, was modified. The fifth question became a "required field" to ensure participants' response before moving to the questionnaire questions and limited responses to one response to overcome participants' choice of more than one classification as experienced in the pilot study.

Although the pilot study did not involve analyzing collected data, the eight participants' feedback was helpful in improving the first-round questionnaire. The pilot study concluded with minor changes to the first round questionnaire (see Appendix C). Changes were related to layout and the required-field option. The pilot study also highlighted the importance of sending the questionnaire through e-mail messages and a personalized questionnaire hyperlink to ensure identification of responses. Upon the completion of the pilot study, recognized experts nominated 200 potential research participants.

Round 1: Open-ended questions. After the conclusion of the pilot study, the actual data collection process started. An e-mail message was sent to invite the 200 nominated potential research participants to join the study (see Appendix C). The invitation included a clear description of the study, time frame, expected role of participants, and informed consent form. Participants were given 2 weeks to respond and submit any inquiries about the study.

As the sample followed the snowball technique, the nomination process stopped after the responses reached the required number (Miles & Huberman, 1994). Nineteen e-email addresses bounced back and were removed from the study. Fifty responses were received, with 10 incomplete questionnaire responses or incomplete informed consent forms. Incomplete responses were ignored. After 1 week, a reminder message was sent to non-respondents. No withdrawals from the study took place.

As the study was conducted in English, all participants were selected and responded accordingly. Responses were expressive and in the context of the study. No language barriers were noted. A response by Edu3 on the fifth question was the only exception. On the same question, Y2 responded "not sure." Due to their expertise level, some participants used technical terms such as "360 degree survey" and "output-based evaluation" under the evaluation tools.

Upon the analysis of the first round responses, 16 themes and 85 subthemes were identified. As the aim of the first round was to elicit rich data from the participants, subthemes with limited frequency (e.g., mentioned only once by one stakeholder) were included in the common themes to ensure diversity of participants' perspectives (see Appendix D). Responses of the first three questions in the Round 1 questionnaire identified the needed competencies for youth development and leadership for Egyptian citizens between the ages of 15 and 24. The themes found included values, leadership, technical knowledge and skills, and personal traits and skills.

Responses varied according to the stakeholders' experiences, nature, age, discipline, and interests. Educators contributed most to skills and contributed least to values. Parents contributed most to personality and contributed least to technical knowledge and skills. Youth contributed most to technical knowledge and skills and contributed least to physical traits and values. Employers contributed most to leadership and contributed least to physical traits. Community leaders contributed most to skills and contributed least to physical traits.

Question 4 of Round 1 asked participants to identify ways or types of opportunities for teaching youth (ages 15–24) leadership competencies. Results included the following themes: family support, education and training methods, education and training content, extracurricular activities, community activities, national and international opportunities, and diversity. Results varied according to the context of each stakeholder.

Under the family support theme, only educators, parents, and community leaders contributed. Under the education and training methodologies, educators contributed the most and parents contributed the least number of inputs. Under education and training content, educators, youth, and community leaders contributed equally. Parents contributed the most input to the education and training content. Under the extracurricular activities, community leaders contributed the most input. Under the community activities, youth and employers scored equally as the highest contribution followed by parents and community leaders. Under national and international opportunities, parents contributed the most input. Educators and youth scored equally as the least input. Under diversity, employers contributed the most input.

Question 5 of Round 1 asked participants how to evaluate effectively leadership opportunities and programs for youth (ages 15–24). The identified themes were assessment, evaluation tools, and long-term impact. The results showed stakeholders' interests and consideration. Under assessment tools, educators contributed the most input and employers the least input. Under evaluation tools, employers contributed the most input and educators contributed the least. Under long-term impact, the community leaders contributed the most input and employers contributed the least input.

The sixth question was an open-ended question that asked participants to list information related to youth leadership not covered in the questionnaire. Responses to the sixth question varied. Nine participants skipped the question, 11 participants responded "nothing to be added," and 20 participants had comments (see Appendix E). Five responses were concerned about the layout of the questionnaire. Three of those five responses suggested a multiple-choice style rather than open-ended questions. Two of the five responses suggested including a definition of leadership, using competencies, and incorporating frameworks in the study. Two participants suggested adding a question about the factors hindering youth leadership. The suggestion was integrated as an open-ended question in the second-round questionnaire. Four responses commented about the roles and responsibilities of different stakeholders in youth leadership development (e.g., media, government). Three responses related to leadership aspects including personal vision and mission, leadership as a responsibility, and inspirational leadership. The comments also included suggestions about evaluation, process of leadership development, and others (e.g., social and financial factors).

Round 2: Likert-type scale. After analyzing the data generated from Round 1, questions for the second round were drafted (see Appendix F).

Round 2 consisted of a multiple-choice questionnaire. The questionnaire questions included all 16 themes and 85 associated subthemes. Participants were requested to rate the expert responses from Round 1 according to the Likert-type scale that included the following categories: 5 = *very important,* 4 = *important,* 3 = *neutral,* 2 = *not very important,* 1 = *not important.* Participants were expected to rate responses according to their opinion on how the responses relate and contribute to the youth leadership development. As some of the participants' comments in Round 1 highlighted the importance of identifying the factors that hinder the development of youth leadership, one open-ended question was added to Round 2.

In the introductory note to Round 2, participants were assured that identification and responses would remain confidential, and the researcher would be the only individual with access to survey results. The online questionnaire was open for responses for 2 weeks. After 1 week, a reminder message was sent to participants who did not respond to the questionnaire.

Twenty-five participants responded to Round 2, for a 62% participation rate. From Round 2 data, the mean was calculated for all subthemes (see Appendix G). Although themes with consensus reaching 80%, equivalent to 4.0 or higher, were considered in writing the third round, consensus about subthemes will be used in developing future youth leadership programs for ages 15 to 24. The identified competencies and skills can be used as selection criteria for potential young leaders or as developmental areas in future programs.

For competencies and skills, all subthemes for values, leadership, physical traits, and skills reached or exceeded the identified benchmark. Under technical knowledge and skills, fundraising and scientific and research skills did not reach consensus. Under personality and emotional aspects, holistic views did not achieve consensus. In developing future programs, subthemes will be considered in a hierarchy according to their mean value. As an example, in the values theme, future programs will consider accepting and respecting others (4.88); ethics and integrity (4.8); fairness, sympathy, and forgiveness (4.44); and family values (4.16). If a future program cannot include all identified values due to time or content constraints, priority will be given to accepting and respecting others, as it had the highest mean value in this category.

For teaching leadership, all subthemes under extracurricular, community activities, and diversity achieved consensus. Financial support under family support, research under education and training methodologies, global affairs under education and training content, and sports/clubs/competitions and civic engagement and political parties under national and international opportunities did not reach consensus. Leadership and skills development (4.64) and independence and responsibility (4.6) under education and training content contributing to the teaching of leadership in youth ages 15–24 scored the highest consensus. Participants' consensus was the lowest in summer jobs and internships, field trips, and following a role model with a mean of (4.08).

Under evaluation of leadership development, consensus was limited. Under the assessment tools theme, out of seven subthemes only end of program's presentation or project (4.16) and assess learning through participants' interaction (4.24) gained consensus. Lack of consensus in the subthemes affected the overall average of the assessment tools negatively and therefore this category was not included in the third round of the Delphi. Under the evaluation tools, five of the 11 subthemes did not reach consensus. Subthemes 360-degree survey, evaluation forms to measure satisfaction level, evaluating program's content in comparison with other countries, and qualitative and quantitative research will not be included as evaluation tools in evaluating future programs for youth leadership development. Under the long-term impact tools, all subthemes gained consensus except for the fast track and high flyers opportunities (3.68). Participants' unfamiliarity with the term may have affected scoring its importance.

The responses for the last open-ended question focused on the factors hindering youth leadership development (see Appendix H). Twenty-one participants responded and four skipped this question. The identified factors with highest frequency of responses were lack of opportunities for learning, researching, training, and exposure; lack of funding and infrastructure required to develop leadership programs; negative family influences and mind-set of parents/adults not believing in youth leadership; and lack of skilled and knowledgeable trainers, coaches, and counselors to discover leadership talents, offer support and mentoring, and provide feedback and guidance.

Round 3: Ranking of identified themes. After the analysis of Round 2 responses and calculation of the mean for each subtheme and average of themes, drafting Round 3 began (see Appendix I). As consensus was based on an average of 4.0 or 80% of agreement among responses, family support (3.92) and assessment tools (3.92) were not included in the third-round survey. The Round 3 questionnaire included four questions. The first three questions requested participants to rank responses in the order that best expressed their opinion as contributors to youth leadership development in the areas of capabilities; skills; and competencies, activities and opportunities, and evaluation procedures. The fourth question requested participants to suggest recommendations to overcome the four factors identified as hindering youth leadership development for the ages 15–24 in Egypt.

The questions did not include the mean value of each theme to avoid influencing the respondents' decision and response. After 1 week, a reminder message was sent to participants who did not respond to the questionnaire. Twenty-six participants responded to Round 3, totaling a 65% participation rate (see Table 5).

Table   5

Response Rate of Respondents for Each Round (Initial n = 40)

Completed round	No. panel members completing responses	% of participation
Round 1	40	100.0
Round 2	25	62.5
Round 3	26	65.0

The first three questions were answered by all 26 participants. In the first question, four participants commented the following: "actually leadership guided by values is key," "these are very difficult to rank with accuracy and confidence," "Youth need to be first qualified as leaders with respectful values before acquiring new skills that will empower their natural aptitude. In some areas of leadership, a young leader needs to be charismatic too," and "I am not sure exactly what is meant by leadership and physical skills. A brief explanation of what each one means could avoid confusion and lead to precise responses." In the second question, one participant commented, "These are also difficult to rank with confidence as they depend a lot on each specific context they are being used in and judged." The third question was related to ranking the procedures contributing to the evaluation process of youth leadership development. One participant commented "same comments as above."

In the last round, participants were asked to rank the themes according to their contribution to youth leadership development. For the identified capabilities, skills, and competencies, participants ranked leadership first and physical traits last. For the activities and opportunities for teaching youth leadership, education and training methodologies, and community service both ranked first. The lowest ranked was education and training content. Participants were concerned more with practical opportunities and request for more interactivity in learning and with the wider society than with knowledge and content. For the evaluation of youth leadership development programs, participants ranked measuring long-term impact first and using evaluation tools second.

The fourth question requested participants to recommend solutions to overcome four factors hindering youth leadership development, which were identified by the research participants in Round 2. The four factors were as follows: (a) lack of opportunities for learning, researching, training, and exposure; (b) lack of funding and infrastructure required to develop leadership programs; (c) negative family influences, mind-set of parents/adults not believing in youth leadership; and (d) lack of skilled and knowledgeable trainers, coaches, and counselors to discover leadership talents, offer support and mentoring, and provide feedback and guidance.

For the first and fourth factors, only 23 participants responded. For the second and third factors, only 24 participants responded. Responses were compiled according to the response sequence and stakeholder classification (see Appendix J). Responses were analyzed to find common recommendations according to the four different factors.

For the first factor, which was the lack of opportunities for learning, researching, training, and exposure, 16 responses suggested the development of and offering more hands-on programs and training through school and university curricula, extracurricular activities, and local communities including nongovernmental organizations and chambers of commerce. Four responses highlighted online education and training as a solution to the lack of opportunities for learning, research, training, and exposure. Four responses suggested international exposure through exchange programs, training, and development agencies. One suggestion focused on the elimination of any attempt to suppress children and youth creativity at an early stage (Y8). Another response suggested promoting apprenticeship degrees rather than academic degrees (P2).

For the second factor, which discussed the lack of funding and infrastructure required to develop leadership programs, nine responses suggested overcoming a lack of funding through local and international donors, fundraising activities, the ability of nongovernmental organizations to use funds efficiently, and the interest of private sector and multinational companies in corporate social responsibility. Four responses suggested integrating youth leadership in school activities and seeking governmental funding through the different institutions (e.g., Ministry of Education, Ministry of Higher Education, National Council for Youth) and nongovernmental support (e.g., Rotary). Two responses suggested the contribution of private schools toward funding public schools through their community service projects (CL6) and mosques hosting and promoting youth leadership development (Edu1). Two responses suggested other emerging factors exist: organization and dedication (Y3) and content and methodology of training and activities (P6). One participant suggested offering micro-financing (P3). Participant Y8 noted the challenge is "to fight any corruption existing in the chain of command in the program."

For the third factor, 12 responses suggested overcoming negative family influences and rigid mind-set of parents/adults not believing in youth leadership through offering awareness programs to parents, whole family, and society. Participants suggested awareness programs to be presented through school programs, nongovernmental organizations, social media, official and private media, publications, training and dialogues with experts and psychologists. Nine responses suggested that offering real opportunities for youth leadership development, sharing success stories of role models of young leaders, integrating leadership mentoring in school activities, and awarding potential leaders will overcome parental and societal negative influence and mind-set toward youth leadership development. Three responses commented about the difficulty overcoming this issue, saying "there is no one size fits all in Egypt" (Y3), "very difficult to change" (CL8), and "this will take time" (CL4). Participant Edu2 noted that stakeholders in the area of youth leadership development need to work harder on the environment to overcome this hindering factor.

For the fourth factor, 14 responses suggested professional development through training and mentoring to trainers, coaches, and counselors working with young leaders to overcome lack of skills and knowledge among them. Four responses suggested developing trainers, coaches, and counselors through recruiting volunteers, training, and offering them adequate opportunities for practice. Three responses suggested considering the overall welfare of trainers, coaches, and counselors (CL4) and certifying workers in the field of youth leadership development through international recognized accrediting bodies (P4 and CL1). Two responses suggested using the online medium for training, mentoring, and development (CL2 and P6).

Research Question 1

The first three questions in the Round 1 questionnaire contributed to RQ1, dealing with needed competencies for youth development and leadership for Egyptian citizens between the ages of 15 and 24. Under RQ1, the themes found included values, leadership, technical knowledge and skills, and personal traits and skills. Few subthemes recorded full contributions from all stakeholders. Under the RQ1 themes, inspiring people to act, vision, firm/disciplined/responsible/credible, optimistic/ambitious/risk taker, objective/flexible/patient, creativity/problem solving/decision making, and presentation/communication were recorded.

In the Round 2 questionnaire, the first 6 themes corresponded to the first research question. Mean value was calculated for all 6 themes and associated subthemes. Under values, the highest mean was for accepting and respecting others (4.88), and the lowest mean was for family values (4.16). Under leadership, the highest mean was for taking initiative and leading projects (4.64), and the lowest mean was for leading by example and self-discovery (4.24). Under technical knowledge and skills, the highest mean was for debating and public speaking (4.44), and the lowest mean was for fundraising (3.52). Under physical traits, the highest mean was for energetic and active (4.72), and the lowest mean was for attractive and presentable (4.00). Under personality and emotions, the highest mean was for confidence and self-esteem; determination, perseverance, and hard working; and firm, disciplined, responsible, and credible (4.72); the lowest mean was for holistic views (3.96). Under skills, the highest mean was for presentation and communication skills (4.56) and the lowest mean was for negotiation skills (4.32).

In Round 3, participants ranked essential capabilities, skills, and competencies in the following order: leadership (57.7%), values (38.5%), skills (34.6%), technical knowledge and skills (30.8%), personality and emotions (26.9%), and physical traits (57.7%) as illustrated in Table 6.

Table   6

Essential Capabilities, Skills, and Competencies

Rank	Identified themes	% of participants
First	Leadership	57.7%
Second	Values	38.5%
Third	Skills	34.6%
Fourth	Technical Knowledge and Skills	30.8%
Fifth	Personality and Emotions	26.9%
Sixth	Physical Traits	57.7%

Research Question 2

In the Round 1 questionnaire, the fourth question contributed to RQ2, which examined needed processes to build and deliver youth development and leadership programs for Egyptian citizens between the ages of 15 and 24. Under RQ2, the themes identified were family support, education and training methodologies, education and training content, extracurricular activities, community activities, national and international opportunities, and diversity. Under the RQ2 themes, the following subthemes recorded full contributions from all stakeholders: hands-on activities and interactive workshop training, meetings/camps/youth summits, conducting social work and community service projects, and sports/clubs/competitions.

In Round 2, the mean value was calculated for the seven identified themes related to the second research question. Under family support, the highest mean was for emotional support (4.36) and the lowest mean was for financial support (3.48). Under education and training methodologies, the highest mean was for quality of formal education (4.48) and the lowest mean was for research (3.88). Under education and training content, the highest mean was for leadership and skills development (4.64) and the lowest mean was for global affairs (3.96). Under extracurricular activities, the highest mean was for meeting, camps, and youth summits (4.52) and the lowest mean was for field trips (4.08). Under community activities, the highest mean was for conducting social work and community service projects (4.44) and the lowest mean was for following a role model (4.08). Under national and international opportunities, the highest mean was for travel, study abroad, and host family stays (4.48) and the lowest mean was for sports, clubs, and competitions (3.88). Under diversity, the highest mean was for exposure to a diversity of views (4.48) and the lowest mean was for participation in a diversity of activities (4.16). In Round 3, participants ranked activities and opportunities that contribute to teaching youth leadership development as follows: community activities (26.9%), education and training methodologies (26.9%), national and international opportunities and activities (26.9%), extracurricular activities (23.1%), and diversity (23.1%) as illustrated in Table 7.

Table   7

Activities and Opportunities that Contribute to Teaching Youth Leadership Development

Rank	Identified themes	% of participants
First	Community activities	26.9
	Education and training methodologies	26.9
Second	National and international opportunities and activities	26.9
Third	Extra-curricular activities	23.1
Fourth	Diversity aspects	23.1
Fifth	Diversity aspects	23.1
Sixth	Education and training content	26.9

Research Question 3

In the Round 1 questionnaire, the fifth question contributed to RQ3, which examined needed evaluative tools to ensure effective implementation of youth development and leadership programs for Egyptian citizens between the ages of 15 and 24. Under RQ3, the identified themes were assessment tools, evaluation tools, and long-term impact. Under the RQ3 themes, no subthemes had a full contribution from all stakeholders. In Round 2, the mean was calculated for the three identified themes. Under assessment tools, the highest mean was for assess learning through participants' interaction (4.24) and the lowest mean was for journals/reflections/reports (3.60). Under evaluation tools, the highest theme was for mentoring and coaching (4.48) and the lowest mean was for evaluation forms to measure satisfaction level (3.52). Under long-term impact, the highest mean was for sustainability (4.48) and the lowest mean was for fast track and high flyers opportunities (3.68). In the last round, participants ranked measuring long term impact first and using evaluation tools second (see Table 8).

Table   8

Procedures Contributing to the Evaluation Process of Youth Leadership
Development

Rank	Identified themes	% of participants
First	Measuring long-term impact	57.7
Second	Using evaluation tools	57.7

Summary

Chapter 4 contained the results and analysis for the collected data through the three Delphi rounds. The presentation began with an illustration of the sample demographics. A pilot study was conducted among eight participants to pretest the first questionnaire. In Round 1, 40 participants responded. Twenty-five participants responded in Round 2, and 26 responded in the last round.

Through an inductive reasoning data analysis method, the qualitative data collected in the first round produced 16 common themes and 85 subthemes that were used as the foundation for designing a 5-point Likert-type scale in Round 2. The importance scale included the following choices: *very important, important, neutral, not very important,* and *not important.* In Round 3, participants were requested to give their feedback and agreement about the data provided in Round 2. Consensus for each question was determined when 80% or more of the panelists were in agreement, which is represented by a weighted mean rating equivalent to or higher than 4.0. To reach final consensus, participants were asked to rank the statements in accordance to the mean responses and narrative feedback from the other participants.

Under the first research question, participants ranked leadership as first and physical traits as last needed competencies for youth development and leadership for Egyptian citizens between the age of 15 and 24. Under the second research question, participants ranked community activities and education and training methodologies as first and education and training content as last needed process to build and deliver youth development and leadership programs for Egyptian citizens between the ages of 15 and 24. Under the third research question, participants ranked measuring long-term impact as first and using evaluation tools as last needed evaluation tools to ensure effective implementation of youth development and leadership programs for Egyptian citizens between the ages of 15 and 24.

Round 2 included an open-ended question about the experts' opinion on factors hindering youth development in Egypt. The identified factors were: (a) lack of opportunities for learning, researching, training, and exposure; (b) lack of funding and infrastructure required to develop leadership programs; (c) negative family influences, mind-set of parents/adults not believing in youth leadership; and (d) lack of skilled and knowledgeable trainers, coaches, and counselors to discover leadership talents, offer support and mentoring, and provide feedback and guidance. In the last round, participants were asked to present suggestions to overcome the factors identified as most frequently hindering youth leadership development.

Chapter 5 includes an interpretive discussion of the results of the modified Delphi study. The analysis incorporates a detailed review of the study results, implications, and relationship to the available literature. Chapter 5 contains conclusions and recommendations for future youth leadership programs and leadership researchers.

Chapter 5: Conclusion and Recommendations

In Egypt, the youth revolution in January 2011 was a tool to express the youth's discontent with exclusion from cultural, political, and civic participation over the past three decades. Youth dream of a new social contract and are eager for empowerment, employment, democracy, and good governance (Handoussa, 2011). Chapter 1 contained an introduction to the topic of the study and its significance to leadership and Egypt's development. The general problem addressed in this study was the lack of adequate opportunities for young adults to develop and practice leadership in Egypt (United Nations Volunteers, 2008). The specific problem was the absence of information and understanding about the youth leadership competencies, processes, and evaluative tools needed to build effective leadership programs (Shokr, 2004). The study was conducted to fill the gap in the knowledge base.

The qualitative study supported by quantitative data with a modified Delphi design involved exploring and identifying the leadership competencies, processes, and evaluative tools needed to develop Egyptian youth leadership programs in the future that will target young adults between the ages of 15 and 24. The purpose of the study was to explore, examine, and refine the leadership skills and competencies needed for young leaders in Egypt; to determine how to develop multiple youth development and leadership opportunities for youth at ages 15–24; and to establish necessary effective evaluative methods. In Round 1 of the Delphi study, 40 participants were asked to answer six seed questions. Responses generated 16 themes and 85 subthemes as the foundation for the second and third rounds. Data collection procedures and analysis were discussed in Chapter 4. Chapter 5 includes further discussion and analysis, conclusions, implications, limitations, and recommendations.

The theoretical framework of the research, which was the developmental contextualization; Dewey's experiential learning; Vygotsky's zone of proximal development; and Bandura's social learning theory, supported the use of the Delphi method and equally the conclusion of the study. Participants and expert panelists identified the needed leadership competencies, processes, and evaluative tools with 80% consensus or higher for developing Egyptian youth leadership programs in the future that target young adults between the ages of 15 and 24. The expert consensus supported Lerner et al.'s (2005), Gruber and Mandl's (2001), and Pelletier and Corter's (2006) adoption of the social ecology or the developmental contextualization theory in youth leadership development.

Research Question 1

The first research question asked what are the needed competencies for youth development and leadership for Egyptian citizens between the ages of 15 and 24. Over the three Delphi rounds, the first question was answered through identifying themes and subthemes, valuing each item in the subthemes, and ranking the themes related to needed competencies. Participants' responses (57.7%) and ranking leadership as first and physical traits as last expressed genuine care for the functional frames of leadership over leaders' characteristics (MacNeil, 2006).

Results from the first round and participants' identification of subthemes under leadership (taking initiative and leading projects; inspiring people to act; strategic thinking, planning, and organizing; adaptive; resolving conflict; leading by example; self-discovery; vision; and managing change) indicated the participants' interest in transformational leadership (Conger, 1999; Heifetz & Laurie, 2003; Tucker & Russell, 2004) rather than the trait theory and personal characteristics (Chary, 2004; Shriberg et al., 2002; Wren, 2004) and transactional leadership (Griffin, 2008; Northouse, 2010). In the current study, the identified competencies overlapped with the leadership competency model (Central Michigan University, 2004), which included "self-management, leading others, task management, innovation, and social responsibility" (p. 5). The generated youth leadership competencies are unique to Egypt's context and the specified age group (15–24). Ranking values in the second rank for the list of competencies and traits a young leader needs to have supported OECD's (2005) call for a movement beyond knowledge and skills and Klau's (2006) recommendations to policy makers and educators for leadership development planning.

Research Question 2

The second research question asked: what are the needed processes to build and deliver youth development and leadership programs for Egyptian citizens between the ages of 15 and 24. Results indicated the participants' interest in youth leadership programs generating youth that can serve others and the community. Results match how servant leadership (Libby et al., 2006; Rogers & Shriberg, 2002) can be fulfilled through changing self, motivating others, developing followers, and satisfying the needs of their communities and people. Consistency in identifying and ranking community activities as the first contributor to youth leadership development supports Klenk's (2002) call for leadership development through context, experience, and leader's contribution.

Stakeholders' insistence to rank education and training methodologies highly supports Cao's (2005) suggestion for motivational instructions using inclusion, entertainment, and edification. Education and training methodologies should eliminate deductive teaching methods and start to follow inductive methods (i.e., project-based learning, case studies, and problem-solving learning; Prince & Felder, 2006). Although many researchers support youth leadership programs that include global issues (Krupp & O'Neill, 2007), participants in the current study did not reach consensus for the integration of global affairs, with a mean of (3.96), in the education and training content. Consensus was considered for mean values equal to or higher than 4.00.

Although the study results did not approach the mechanics of youth leadership development from a management standpoint, the results included a long list of activities and opportunities that can guide educators, trainers, coaches, and counselors in the development of youth leadership programs in Egypt for youth ages 15–24. Process orientation can be adopted from Leskiw and Singh's (2007) model for an effective leadership development process: needs assessment, selection of proper audience, design of apt infrastructure, learning system, an evaluation system, and rewarding success and improving deficiencies. Process orientation should include attraction, development, and retention of leaders at all levels (Krupp & O'Neill, 2007). According to

Ricketts and Rudd (2002), youth leadership development has three stages: awareness, interaction, and mastery.

Research Question 3

The third research question asked: what are the needed evaluative tools to ensure effective implementation of youth development and leadership programs for Egyptian citizens between the ages of 15 and 24. To ensure effective evaluation and the adoption of a participatory approach, stakeholders' participation in planning and performance of the evaluation is vital (Michie, 2001). The results reflected how the participants focused on program evaluation, output/performance measurement, and impact (Powell, 2006). Participants agreed on using outcome and process evaluations (Wholey et al., 2004). None of the responses referred to the cost-effectiveness evaluation (Canton & Hancock, 2007). Through the identification of evaluation subthemes in Round 1 and calculating mean values according to Round 2 responses, the results indicated participants' interest in evaluating leadership programs' effect on youth (e.g., mentoring and coaching with a mean value of 4.48) rather than evaluation in relation to resources and process (e.g., evaluation forms to measure satisfaction level with a mean value of 3.52). Responses suggested the use of formative and summative evaluation (Gordon, 2004).

In future youth leadership development programs, evaluation should be planned and integrated at the design stage to ensure the satisfaction of all stakeholders' questions (Canton & Hancock, 2007). Evaluation should involve assessing the planned objectives, selection criteria for youth, and program activities. If youth leadership programs will use rubrics as a method for evaluation, the rubrics should contain levels of mastery, commentaries, and descriptions of consequences (Huba & Freed, 2000). Rubrics should also include evaluators' suggestions for individual developmental plans and any personal reflections of the participating youth.

Limitations

The current study included a number of limitations. First, generalizations may not be possible. The sample size of 40 invited experts represented five different identified stakeholder groups: educators, parents, youth (19–24 years old), employers, and community leaders. Although the five categories represented the major stakeholders involved in youth leadership, the categories and sample size did not represent all stakeholders influencing youth leadership development and implementation. Other stakeholders that could have been included in the research are sport coaches and scout leaders.

The results may not be generalized due to the small number of the sample size compared to the overall population of Egypt and specifically the greater Cairo area where the research took place. Limiting the research to greater Cairo and urban locations did not give any opportunity for interested experts to participate from other locations outside greater Cairo. The study was not able to represent the rural population in Egypt, which represents 67% of the total population (CIA, 2009), and its culture, needs, and progress.

All participants in the study were expected to possess a bachelor's degree or higher and have an adequate English language proficiency, and all participants fulfilled the degree requirements and English language proficiency. Between 2005 and 2008, Egypt's illiteracy rate reached 44% (United Nations International Children's Emergency Fund, 2010). For generalization in future studies, the education level, and proficiency of English language should not be a requirement for participation.

Although the study included five governorates, which were Cairo, Giza, Helwan, Sixth of October, and El Qualubia, two governorates were canceled due to the political changes that Egypt experienced after the January 25th Revolution in 2011. The study was not affected as participants filled the demographic question based on the earlier governmental classification. Egypt has 27 governorates. The governorates covered in the current study represented only 18.5% of the total capacity of Egypt.

Second, lack of clarity or definitions may have confused the participants. During the first round questionnaire, participants were expected to fill a demographic section. The last question in the demographics was stakeholder classification. Wording used in the definition of community leaders (as part of the stakeholder) confused some participants. The use of the word *leader* deterred many respondents from choosing it because of its cultural connotation to political or societal positions or recognition. Five participants (out of eight) called to check if they would qualify for such a category. In the first round and under the sixth question, two responses indicated a need to include a clear definition of leadership, competencies used, and framework used in this research. In the third-round survey, two participants commented that theme ranking had been difficult without the presentation of a clear definition and a relevant context to each theme. Participants had the opportunity to offer feedback only in the first and third round. The second round was limited to the scale of importance and did not include the opportunity for offering narrative feedback except for the last question.

Third, logistics for sending the questionnaires included some challenges. The e-mail user name (progress2005) was not indicative of the researcher's identity; therefore, many nominated participants did not consider the e-mail message important. Reminder messages were sent during the three rounds. The timing of Round 1 may not have been appropriate as it aligned with final exams. Educators, parents, and youth stakeholders' best interest was not considered. Communication with respondents took longer than planned.

The fourth limitation related to the large number of themes and subthemes. Although the first questionnaire tried to generate a rich qualitative response from the participants, the 16 themes and 85 subthemes affected the duration of the data analysis and response rate in the second questionnaire due to the time needed to evaluate and rank 85 items according to importance. Data collection lasted for 9 months, which is longer than the 3 months originally planned for (Cuhls, 2003).

Implications

Research studies benefit a number of stakeholders in the process of decision and policy making (Creswell, 2005). Although the current study included five stakeholder groups, the benefits of the study are not limited to them. The following sections include a discussion on the study implications and associated stakeholders.

Youth leadership programs. Youths' physical traits, cognition, and emotion need to be considered during the development of youth leadership programs. Future programs should follow the youth development theory, which is based on three basic theories of child development and learning: Dewey's experiential learning (Dewey, 1938), Vygotsky's zone of proximal development, and Bandura's social learning theory (Learning Theories Knowledgebase, 2009). Chung (2005) warned stakeholders that utilizing available theoretical resources and combining them creatively may not be enough to develop effective programs. Programs should be built on available knowledge with adequate flexibility and understanding of the youth. Successful leaders are expected to have the following characteristics: knowledge, competency, and character. Youth leadership program should select young adults (15–24) with potential leadership traits and willingness to learn and build effective programs that would integrate the minds, senses, and hearts of the youth.

To develop whole leaders, future youth leadership development programs in Egypt should develop both intrapersonal and interpersonal relationships and consider competencies and skills through a paradigm of complexity, diversity, and uncertainty (Herzog, 2007). In future youth leadership programs, complexity leveling should consider adopting Tubbs and Schulz's (2006) three-level model: the individual's core personality level, the individual's values, and the individual's leadership behaviors and skills. Jennings et al. (2006) suggested critical youth empowerment, which is a conceptual framework centered on the foundation of integrating youth empowerment processes and outcomes at both the individual and the collective levels. The results of the study contribute to the individual and collective levels. Leadership developers need to consider skills, experiences, needs, motivation, and cumulative effort (Kress, 2006). Youth leadership programs need to occur over a prolonged duration to ensure the cumulative effect of the diversified experiences of the young leaders.

The results in Round 2 indicated youth leadership programs should consider youth's participation in a variety of activities (mean 4.16), exposure to a diversity of views (mean 4.48), and freedom of expression (mean 4.40). Diversity of activities and views should be considered in planning future programs. Through mentoring and coaching (which had a mean value of 4.48 in Round 2 results and ranked first in evaluation tools in the third-round results), program objectives can be monitored even after the program's completion.

Role of youth in leadership development. In the current study, youth (19–24 years old) served as an effective stakeholder group, supporting Libby et al.'s (2006) concept of positive youth–adult partnerships. Youth leadership programs should incorporate a youth-oriented approach in the process of planning, developing, delivering, and evaluating the programs (Saunders, 2002). When approaching leadership development, trainers need to consider people's strengths and leverage them, taking into account the whole leader (Krupp & O'Neill, 2007). Youth are an excellent resource and would be the best to assess youth needs. Youth can assist as objects, recipients, resources, and partners. Conner and Strobel (2007) found that youth can have a role and affect the developmental context that shaped them. Youth can affect youth leadership developmental programs positively (Brown Urban, 2008). In Round 3, participants (17%) suggested considering youth in the long-term plan of preparing qualified leaders to serve in the field of youth leadership development.

Trainers, coaches, and counselors for developing youth leadership. Effective teachers and youth caregivers need to use their understanding and experience in the utilization of background knowledge, learning styles, multiple intelligences, brain and learning connections, and special needs to plan effective activities for teaching and learning. Leadership development programs should entail continuous learning and growing through using curricula-based and didactic approaches to include more experiential and context-based approaches with a focus on community-based initiatives.

Trainers, coaches, and counselors should be equipped and ready to use a variety of approaches and techniques to reach planned objectives in youth leadership programs. Trainers, coaches, and counselors need specialized education and continuous training that would equip them to develop future leaders (DuBois et al., 2003). To be able to recognize youth's optimal zone, youth leadership programs and decision makers should get to know the youth and surrounding environments. Responsible professionals running youth leadership programs should study and consider different factors that influence youth and might affect their leadership development, as discussed in Chapter 2 (e.g., adolescence, education, political, economic, social, religious, and theoretical factors).

In the third round, results reflected that the welfare of professionals working in the field of youth leadership development should be a priority. Seventy percent of the participants suggested focusing on trainers, coaches, and counselors through continuous professional development and mentorship. To give credibility to the profession, three participants suggested certifying trainers, coaches, and counselors through international accrediting agencies.

Recommendations

Egyptian society's perception about youth's ability needs to change and consider a more active role for youth participation and leadership development through different paths as suggested by 87.5% of the participants in the third round. Youth should be encouraged and supported by all societal sectors, stakeholders, and decision makers as noted by 50% of the participants in the last round. Youth leadership programs should have multiple channels and welcome youth participation through political, cultural, social, and economic empowerment. This section will include recommendations generated from the study's results. Recommendations will be to leaders and stakeholders in the field of youth leadership development, and recommendations for future research.

118

Recommendations to leaders and stakeholders. Any past experiences and learned lessons in the area of youth leadership development should be studied and utilized. Stakeholders should consider capitalizing on the Egyptian experience from the 1960s through the Youth Socialism Institute, which supported five principles: the integration between intellectual development and the practice of leadership skills, leadership development through in-house accommodation in a series of overnight camps, continuous assessment and evaluation of the participants' progress in public activities, integration in the public community work and leadership training, and open discussion and debates to encourage the young leaders' self-expression. The institute's program included three levels of leadership development, community development activities, and public service and a variety of experiences to broaden the political, economic, and social awareness of the members. The Youth Socialism Institute's content and delivery methods should be adjusted to suit 21st-century competencies and needs. The new version of the institute should consider aligning the new global trends in human skills development with local needs, culture, and context. To ensure young leaders receive adequate opportunities for practice, leadership development programs should be offered in different levels and on a continuous basis (Day, 2000). Based on the participants' identification of essential capabilities, skills, and competencies (leadership, personality and emotions, physical traits, skills, technical knowledge and skills, and values) contributing to youth leadership development in Round 1 responses and associated with highest mean values in Round 2, future programs in youth leadership development should adopt a holistic approach to include the emotional, physical, and intellectual needs of youth (Oyserman, 2001). In the last round, 70% of the participants suggested hands-on programs and training, school-based activities and extracurricular activities, and community-related activities.

Youth policy in Egypt is another area that needs extensive focus and development in the near future. Current youth policies entail many difficulties including lack of collaboration between stakeholders in setting and implementing youth policies, lack of trust between young people and governmental authorities, and rising unemployment rates especially among young adults (Youth Partnership, 2005). A participatory approach should be adopted to ensure the inclusion of all voices and views in developing youth in Egypt (Kennedy, 2004). In the last round, participants (38%) noted the importance of collaboration between different stakeholders (e.g., local and international funders, nongovernmental organizations, private sector and multinational companies) to overcome the lack of funding and the infrastructure required to develop leadership programs. A national committee can consist of representatives of governmental organizations working in the field of youth welfare (e.g., Ministry of Education, National Council of Youth, Ministry of Culture, Cultural Palaces, sporting clubs, and Ministry of Population). Discussing and planning youth issues and development should also include all stakeholders, including the five segments included in this study: educators, parents, youth, employers, and community leaders. As discussed in Chapter 2, regional and international exchange of best practices and innovation in the area of youth policy development and implementation should be encouraged for continuous learning. Current youth policies should be revised according to the new changes encountered in Egypt after the Arab Spring of 2011; suggestions listed in the *Human Development Report of 2010* with a special focus on youth (UNDP, 2010); and above all the youth needs and aspirations for equal opportunities, economic empowerment, and a better future.

The Ministry of Education should adopt leadership as a concept and practice for an introduction through formal and informal education to youth at the age of 15 years old, which is equivalent to the last year in middle or preparatory school. The Ministry of Education and Ministry of Higher Education should build channels of communication and cooperation to continue offering leadership programs through school and university-level education. Based on the responses in the last round, participants ranked community activities and education and training methodologies as first in the activities and opportunities that contribute to teaching youth leadership development. New curriculum design should encourage exposure to diverse views and focus on inquiry, critical thinking, and character building. New curriculum designs should integrate community serving activities. This effort should be implemented in both public and private educational institutions to ensure a new cadre of leaders in different disciplines. For the informal education component, nongovernmental organizations and community service organizations can be invited to contribute through their innovative cost effective programs. Youth leadership development programs should abide by and serve the national developmental plan for Egypt to ensure the integration and complementing of efforts. In the last round, 38% of participants suggested integrating leadership in school activities.

Youth leadership development should not follow traditional methods and search for modern means to offer unique opportunities for youth participation and engagement (e.g., youth philanthropy, policy advocacy, and action research). Youth leadership programs should embrace the development of youth-friendly environments, hands-on leadership opportunities, advancement of life skills, and promotion of identity and individuality (Conner & Strobel, 2007). To suit different needs, ages, and segments of youth, processes in youth leadership development programs should be youth oriented using different paths, approaches, and strategies.

Recommendation for future research. The current research has the potential to contribute significantly to the area of youth leadership development for youth ages 15–24 years in Egypt. Future researchers might use the study as baseline information and consensus among different stakeholders on needed competencies, effective processes and opportunities, and evaluation tools for the development of successful youth leadership programs. The study can benefit different segments of society, including educators, social researchers, policy makers, parents, nongovernmental agencies, and funding agencies for the development of leadership programs for youth (ages 15–24) in the future. For leadership research and studies, the results of the study may be helpful for youth leaders and educators to design, establish, and assess youth leadership programs through formal or informal educational activities. The body of research contributes to the area of leadership studies and youth development and can serve as a model for additional studies. The study provided a foundation of information that can contribute to the change of perception and application about Egyptian youth empowerment and leadership from rehabilitation and preventive measures toward development and educational priority.

Based on participants' suggestions (in response to the sixth question in the first round and recommendations in the third round), future research might extend the study of youth leadership to new geographical regions, topics, and research areas; voice the underserved or less represented samples in the community; and benefit leaders, practitioners, and policy makers. The role of government, nongovernmental organizations, and media in youth leadership development is another topic for future research. The future study might contribute to new understanding and practices in youth empowerment and leadership in developing countries. Future research might also include practical models of youth leadership programs for cultural validation, implementation, and evaluation in other countries in the MENA region.

Future research can include the same aspects of this study; including leadership competencies, process, and evaluation, but for other youth segments or ages (e.g., youth at technical institutes and age groups younger than 15 or older than 24 years old). Future studies can consider youth with special needs (e.g., physical, educational). Future research can also consider youth leadership in Egypt in relationship to gender and if there are any differences in leadership styles among young male and female leaders (as indicated in responses to the fifth question in Round 1).

After examining the best practices in Egypt, regionally, and internationally in Chapter 2, future research may be necessary to examine whether youth leadership programs in international environments are based on similar competencies, are basic youth leadership programs portable from country to country, and, if not, what influences the distinctions from country to country. To overcome the generalization concern in the current study and the unrepresentative sample, future research can be carried out to generalize the findings for Egypt or the MENA region or other regions. Further studies might be necessary to explore the possibility of implementing the study results in different geographic areas.

Conclusion

The current qualitative Delphi study was a response to the World Bank's (2007) call for a specialized study to explore youth development in Egypt and Libby et al.'s (2006) suggestion to research the area of effective youth leadership development practices and its components. The study contributed to the knowledge and practice of youth leadership development for youth ages 15–24 in Egypt. As introduced in Chapter 1, the general problem guiding the Delphi study was the lack of adequate opportunities for young adults to develop and practice leadership in Egypt. A gap between the literature available in developed nations and practical application in Egypt or other developing nations in the area of youth leadership development was identified. Research has not identified youth leadership programs but contributed to the understanding to develop effective youth leadership programs in the future for youth ages 15–24 in Egypt.

The theoretical framework of the research, which was based on the developmental contextualization; Dewey's experiential learning; Vygotsky's zone of proximal development; and Bandura's social learning theory, supported the use of the Delphi method and equally the conclusion of the study. The expert consensus supported Lerner et al.'s (2005), Gruber and Mandl's (2001), and Pelletier and Corter's (2006) adoption of the social ecology or the developmental contextualization theory in youth leadership development. In addition, the conclusions conclude effective collaboration among various stakeholder groups to initiate and support youth leadership development.

Results generated over the Delphi iterations responded to the research questions. The first research question asked what are the needed competencies for youth development and leadership for Egyptian citizens between the ages of 15 and 24. Participants ranked leadership as first, values as second, skills as third, technical knowledge and skills as fourth, personality and emotions as fifth, and physical traits as last. The generated youth leadership competencies are unique to Egypt's context and the specified age group (15–24).

The second research question asked: what are the needed processes to build and deliver youth development and leadership programs for Egyptian citizens between the ages of 15 and 24. Results indicated participants' identification and ranking community activities and education and training methodologies as the first contributor to youth leadership development. Participants ranked national and international opportunities and activities as second, extra curricula activities as third, diversity as fourth and fifth, and education and training content as last.

The third research question asked: what are the needed evaluative tools to ensure effective implementation of youth development and leadership programs for Egyptian citizens between the ages of 15 and 24. The results reflected how the participants focused on program evaluation (formative and summative), output/performance measurement, and impact. Participants ranked measuring long term impact as first, and using evaluation tools as second.

The modified Delphi study was intended to identify leadership competencies, processes, and evaluative tools for enforcing leadership as a relational process to build effective leadership programs for youth ages 15–24. The experts provided data through consensus and ranking to answer the research questions and identify leadership competencies, processes, and evaluative tools to construct effective youth leadership programs in the near future. The implications of the results affect the consideration of youth leadership programs; the role of youth in leadership development; and trainers, coaches, and counselors for developing youth leadership for youth ages 15–24. The results from the study had limitations and recommendations for future research, including generalization, the structure of the questionnaire and lack of specific definitions of terms, logistics related to data collection, and a large number of themes and subthemes.

The recommendation to leaders and stakeholders suggested capitalizing on Egypt's experience in the 1960s with the Youth Socialism Institute, revising the youth policies and adopting a participatory approach to include all stakeholders, adopting leadership in formal and informal education in school and college levels, and using nontraditional programs and activities to ensure youth engagement and active participation in youth leadership programs. The recommendations for future leadership research might ensure the optimization of youth participation to voice their needs and views about various aspects related to their development and progress.

Youth are a vital stakeholder and resource that should not be eliminated or marginalized, as has occurred in the past few decades in Egypt. The Arab Spring in 2011 has uncovered the level of oppression young men and women have suffered and the untapped potential that youth still hold. Youth leadership development can contribute to nation building of many uprising countries. Youth are the partners, owners, and leaders for tomorrow's construction.

References

Aaker, D. A., Kumar, V., & Day, G. S. (2007). *Marketing research* (9th ed.). Hoboken, NJ: Wiley.

Abdelhaleem, M. T., & Seymour, D. (1994). Effective leadership in the construction industry. *Engineering Science, 7*, 163-173. Retrieved from http://digital.library.ksu.edu.sa/V7M96R947.pdf

Adler, M., & Ziglio, E. (1996). *Gazing into the oracle: The Delphi method and its application to social policy and public health.* London, England: Jessica Kingsley.

African Leadership Academy. (2010). *Welcome to the ALA Web site.* Retrieved from http://www.africanleadershipacademy.org/site/index.html

Alexander, D. C. (2004). A Delphi study of the trends or events that will influence the Future of California charter schools. *Digital Abstracts International, 65*(10), 3629. (UMI No. 3150304)

Alexander, J. R. (2006). From the president. *Leadership in Action, 26*(3), 2.

Al-Ghanim, M., Al-Zeini, D., Hanafi, C. B., Shasho, S., & Younes, L. (2005). *Arab youth and WPAY, challenges and success 1995-2005: A regional overview.* Retrieved from http://www.un.org/esa/socdev/unyin /documents/wpaysubmissions/gyan_arab_region.pdf

American Chamber of Commerce. (2008). *The report: Emerging Egypt 2008.* Cairo, Egypt: Oxford Business Group.

American Chamber of Commerce in Egypt. (2007). *Egypt–U.S. relations profile.* Retrieved from http://www.amcham-egypt.org

American Heritage dictionary of the English language (4th ed.). (2002). Boston, MA: Houghton Mifflin. Retrieved from http://www.thefreedictionary.com/

American Psychological Association. (2002). *APA publication manual* (5th ed.). Washington DC: Author.

American Psychological Association. (2010). *APA publication manual* (6th ed.). Washington DC: Author.

Anna Lindh Foundation. (2009). *Project case studies.* Retrieved from http://www.euromedalex.org/case-studies

Argyris, C. (2000). *Flawed advice and the management trap.* New York, NY: Academic Press.

Assaad, R., & Barsoum, G. (2007). *Youth exclusion in Egypt: In search of second chances.* Dubai, UAE: Dubai School of Government.

Assaad, R., & Roudi-Fahimi, F. (2007). *Youth in the Middle East and North Africa: Demographic opportunity or challenge?* Retrieved from http://www.prb.org/pdf07/YouthinMENA.pdf

Association Internationale des Etudiants en Sciences Economiques et Commerciales. (2006). *About AISEC.* Retrieved from http://www.aiesec.org/cms/aiesec/AI/About/

Australia Youth Development Association. (2010). *Home.* Retrieved from http://www.aydp.com/

Avolio, B. J., Bass, B. M., & Jung, D. I. (1999). Re-examining the components of transformational and transactional leadership using the multifactor leadership questionnaire. *Journal of Occupational and Organizational Psychology, 72,* 441- 462.

Azarva, J. (2006). Dissident watch: Muhammad al-Sharqawi. *Middle East Quarterly, 13*(4), 96-105.

Babbie, E. (2007). *The practice of social research* (11th ed.). Belmont, CA: Thompson Learning.

Baker, J., Lovell, K., & Harris, N. (2006). How expert are the experts? An exploration of
the concept of "expert" within Delphi panel techniques. *Nurse Researcher, 14,* 59-70.

Banerji, P., & Krishnan, V. R. (2000). Ethical preferences of transformational leaders: An empirical investigation. *Leadership & Organization Development Journal, 21*(8), 405-411.

Barber, A., & Korbanka, J. (2003). *Research and statistics for the social sciences.* Boston, MA: Pearson Custom.

Bayers, J. J. (2004). *Expectancy theory: A universal approach.* Duluth, MN: College of St. Scholastica.

BC Assessment. (2009). *How to prepare for an interview appraisal assistant (clerical) selection process.* Retrieved from http://www.docstoc.com/docs/2289521/What-is-a-competency

Beautiful minds: Think EQ not IQ. (2004). *New Zealand Management, 51,* 11.

Beinecke, R., & Spencer, J. (2007). International leadership, competencies, and issues. *International Journal of Leadership in Public Services*, *3*(3), 4-14.

Bergmann, H. (1999). Introducing a grass-roots model of leadership. *Strategy & Leadership, 27*(6), 15-20.

Bernard, H. R. (2000). *Social research methods: Qualitative and quantitative approaches.* Thousand Oaks, CA: Sage.

Black, L. L., & Magnuson, S. (2005). Women of spirit: Leaders in the counseling profession. *Journal of Counseling and Development: JCD, 83*, 337-343.

Bolden, R., & Gosling, J. (2006). Leadership competencies: Time to change the tune? *Leadership, 2,* 14-163. doi:10.1177/1742715006062932

Bolman, L. G., & Deal, T. E. (2003). Reframing leadership. In Jossey-Bass (Ed.), *Business leadership: A Jossey Bass reader* (pp. 86–110). San Francisco, CA: Jossey-Bass.

Boseman, G. (2008). Effective leadership in a changing world. *Journal of Financial Service Professionals, 62*(3), 36-38.

British Broadcasting Corporation. (2005). *Egypt's Mubarak appeals to voters: Egyptian President Hosni Mubarak has appealed for voters to back his efforts to introduce democratic reforms.* Retrieved from http://news.bbc.co.uk/2/hi/middle_east/4214954.stm

British Council. (2005). *National standards skills project.* Retrieved from http://www.britishcouncil.org/development-education-experience-egypt-national-skills-standards.pdf

Brockman, M. S., Tepper, K., & MacNeil, C. (2007). *Building partnerships for youth.* Retrieved from http://cals-cf.calsnet.arizona.edu/fcs/content.cfm?content=leadership

Brown, C. (2007). The opt-in/opt-out feature in a multi-stage Delphi method study. *International Journal of Social Research Methodology, 10*, 135-144. doi:10.1080/13645570701334084

Brown Urban, J. (2008). Components and characteristics of youth development programs: The voices of youth-serving policymakers, practitioners, researchers, and adolescents. *Applied Developmental Science, 12*(3), 128-139. doi:10.1080/10888690802199400

Bucknall, J. (2001). *The tones of Delphi algorithms and data structures.* Plano, TX: Woodware.

Campbell, D. J. (2007). Establishing a competency model for e-learning instructional *systems designers in the United States* (Doctoral dissertation). Available from ProQuest Dissertations and Theses database. (UMI No. 3302632)

Canton, R., & Hancock, D. (Eds.). (2007). *Dictionary of probation and offender management.* Orlando, FL: Willan.

Cantu, M. (2003). *Mastering Delphi 7.* Alameda, CA: SYBEX.

Cao, K. X. (2005). Three levels of motivation in instruction: Building interpersonal relations with learners. *Distance Learning, 2*(4), 1-7.

Cawthon, D. L. (1992). Leadership and destiny: Expanding our horizons. *Business Forum, 17*(4), 9-12.

Center for Development and Population Activities. (2009). *Celebrating youth around the world.* Retrieved from http://www.cedpa.org /content /news/detail/1672

Central Intelligence Agency. (2009). *World fact book: Egypt.* Retrieved from https://www.cia.gov /library/publications/the-world-factbook/geos/eg.html

Central Intelligence Agency. (2010). *Egypt people 2010.* Retrieved from http://www.theodora.com/wfbcurrent/egypt/egypt_people.html

Central Michigan University. (2004). *Leadership competency model.* Retrieved from http://www.chsbs.cmich.edu/leader_model/CompModel/EDUMAIN.htm

Champion, D. (2006). *Research methods for criminal justice and criminology* (3rd ed.). Upper Saddle River, NJ: Prentice Hall.

Chary, S. N. (2004, March 1). A new perspective on leadership. *Journal of Academy of Business and Economics, 3.* Retrieved from http://www.allbusiness.com/human-resources/employee-development-leadership/300406-1.html

Chaw, A. P. C., Yung, E. H. K., Lam, P. T. I., Tam, C. M., & Cheung, S. O. (2001). Application of Delphi method in selection of procurement systems for construction projects. *Construction Management and Economics, 19,* 699-718.

Chung, C. J. (2005). Theory, practice, and the future of developmental education. *Journal of Developmental Education, 28*(3), 2-10. doi:10.1080/01446190110066128

Clark, D. (2008). *Competencies.* Retrieved from http://www.nwlink.com/~Donclark /hrd/case/competencies.html

Clark, G. (2001). *Student leadership and higher education: A review of the literature* (Doctoral dissertation, University of Southern California). Retrieved from http://asstudents.unco.edu/students /AE-Extra/2004/4/index.html

Clawson, J. G. (2008). *Level three leadership: Getting below the surface* (3rd ed.). Upper Saddle River, NJ: Prentice Hall.

Clayton, M. (1997). Delphi: A technique to harness expert opinion for critical decision-making tasks in education. *Educational Psychology, 17,* 373-387.

Column, S. (2003). *The essence of leadership.* Retrieved from http://hbswk.hbs.edu/archive/3640.html

Communication Initiative Network. (2004). *Youth leadership development initiative(YLDI)–United States.* Retrieved from http://www.comminit.com/en/node123740

Cone, J. D., & Foster, S. L. (1993). *Dissertations and thesis from start to finish.* Washington, DC: American Psychological Association.

Conger, J. A. (1999). Charismatic and transformational leadership in organizations: An insider's perspective on these developing streams of research. *Leadership Quarterly, 10*, 145-179.

Conner, J. O., & Strobel, K. (2007). Leadership development: An examination of individual and programmatic growth. *Journal of Adolescent Research, 22*, 275-297. doi:10.1177/0743558407299698

Cooper, D. R., &Schindler, P. S. (2006). *Business research methods* (9th ed.). New York, NY: McGraw-Hill.

Council for Secular Humanism. (2008). *Secular humanism*. Retrieved from http://www.secularhumanism.org

Creating Minds. (2008). *Delphi method*. Retrieved from http://creatingminds.org/tools /delphi.htm

Creative Youth Leadership Program. (2009). *An overview*. Retrieved from http://creativeyouthleadership.org/index.html

Creswell, J. (2009). *Research design: Qualitative, quantitative, and mixed methods*
approaches (3rd ed.). Los Angeles, CA: Sage.

Creswell, J. (2005). *Educational research: Planning, conducting, and evaluating quantitative and qualitative research*. Upper Saddle River, NJ: Pearson.

Creswell, J. & Miller, D. (2000). Determining validity in qualitative inquiry. *Theory into Practice, 39*(3), 124-131.

Cuhls, K. (2003). *Delphi method*. Retrieved from http://www.unido.org/fileadmin/import/16959_DelphiMethod.pdf

Custer, R. L., Scarcella, J. A., & Stewart, B. R. (1999). The modified Delphi technique: A rotational modification. *Journal of Vocational and Technical Education, 15*(2), 1-11. Retrieved from http://coe.csusb.edu/scarcella/jvte.html

Day, D. V. (2000). Leadership development: A review in context. *The Leadership Quarterly, 11*, 581-613.

Denzin, N. K. (2002). The interpretive process. In M. A. Huberman & M. B. Miles (Eds.). *The qualitative researcher's companion* (pp. 349-366). Newbury Park, CA: Sage.

Denzin, N. K., & Lincoln, Y. S. (Eds.). (2000). *Handbook of qualitative research* (2nd ed.). Thousand Oaks, CA: Sage.

Denzin, N. K., Lincoln, Y. S., & Giardina, M. D. (2006). Disciplining qualitative research. *International Journal of Qualitative Studies in Education, 19*, 769-782.

De Vaus, D. (2006). *Research design in social research*. Thousand Oaks, CA: Sage.

Dewey, J. (1938). *Experience and education*. New York, NY: Touchstone.

Drury, M. L., & Kitsopoulos, S. C. (2005). Do you still believe in the seven deadly myths? *Consulting to Management, 16*, 28-32.

DuBois, D., Lockerd, E. M., Reach, K., & Parra, G. R. (2003). Effective strategies for esteem-enhancement: What do young adolescents have to say? *Journal of Early Adolescence, 23*, 405-434. doi:10.1177/0272431603258346

Duffield, C. (1993). The Delphi technique: A comparison of results obtained using two expert panels. *International Journal of Nursing Studies, 30*, 227-237. doi:10.1016/0020-7489(93)90033-Q

Economist Intelligence Unit. (2009). *Egypt: Country overview*. Retrieved fromhttp://www.eiu.com/

Edelman, A., Gill, P., Comerford, K., Larson, M., & Hare, R. (2004) *Youth development & youth leadership*. Washington, DC: Institute for Educational Leadership.

Egypt State Information Service. (2006a). *State's efforts to protect children*. Retrieved from http://www2.sis.gov.eg/En/Society/Children/efforts/090301000000000001.htm

Egypt State Information Service. (2006b). *Youth and sport*. Retrieved from http://www.sis.gov.eg /En/Pub/yearbook/2006/110104000000000020.htm

Egypt State Information Service. (2010). *Egypt*. Retrieved from http://www.sis.gov.eg

Egyptian International Economic Forum. (2009). *Research*. Retrieved from http://www.eieforum.org /en/index.php#

El Issawy, I. H. (2005). Futures studies and project Egypt 2020. *Futures Research Quarterly, 21*(2), 51-65. Retrieved from http://d.wanfangdata.com.cn /NSTLQK_NSTL_QK10872191.aspx

Ervin, N. E. (2002). *Advanced community health nursing practice: Population-focused care.* Upper Saddle River, NJ: Prentice Hall.

Essex, N. L. (2005). *School law and the public schools: A practical guide for educational leaders* (2nd ed.). Boston, MA: Allyn & Bacon.

Falola, T., & Lerner, R. M. (2004). *Teen life in Africa.* Santa Barbara, CA: Greenwood.

Farag, F. (2007, January 18-24). Chronicles of an uprising: Long shadow cast by the 1977 uprising. *Al Ahram Weekly,* 828. Retrieved from http://weekly.ahram.org.eg/2007/828/special.htm

Festa, P. (2003). *U.N. finds wide digital divide.* Retrieved from http://news.cnet.com/2100-1038_3-5110176.html

Flick, U. (2009). *An introduction to qualitative research* (4th ed.). Thousand Oaks, CA: Sage.

Forsythe, N., Korzeniewicz, R. P., Majid, N., Weathers, G., & Durrant, V. (2003). *Gender inequalities, economic growth and economic reform: A preliminary longitudinal evaluation.* Retrieved from http://www.ilo.org/public/english/employment/strat/download/ep45.pdf

Franklin, K. K., & Hart, J. K. (2006). Idea generation and exploration: Benefits and limitations of the policy Delphi research method. *Innovative Higher Education, 31,* 237-246. doi:10.1007/s10755-006-9022-8

Fraser, M. (1996). *Aggressive behavior in childhood and early adolescence: An ecological-developmental perspective on youth violence.* Retrieved from http://ssw.unc.edu/jif/makingchoices/Publications/Aggressive%20Beha vior/SW--Fraser--1996.pdf

Furash, E. (2003). Leadership = culture. *RMA Journal, 12*(4), 86-91.

Galal, A. (2008, April 17-23). Road not traveled. *El Ahram Weekly.* Retrieved from http://weekly.ahram.org.eg/print/2008/893/sc0131.htm

Galloway, A. (2005). Non-probability sampling. In K. Kempf-Leonard (Ed.), *Encyclopedia of social measurement* (Vol. 2, pp. 859-864). Amsterdam, Netherlands: Elsevier.

Garrod, B. (2008). *The Delphi technique.* Retrieved from http://users.aber.ac.uk/bgg/delphimethod.ppt

Genzuk, M. (2003).*A synthesis of ethnographic research.* Los Angeles, CA: Center for Multilingual, Multicultural Research, University of Southern California.

Glaser, B. G., & Strauss, A. L. (1967). *The discovery of grounded theory: Strategies for qualitative research.* Chicago, IL: Aldine.

Golafshani, N. (2003). Understanding reliability and validity in qualitative research. *The Quality Report, 8*(4), 597-607. Retrieved from http://www.nova.edu/ssss/QR/QR8-4/golafshani.pdf

Goleman, D. (2004). Never stop learning. *Harvard Business Review, 82*, 28-29.

Gong, R. (2005). The essence of critical thinking. *Journal of Developmental Education, 28*(3), 40-41.

Gordon, S. P. (2004). *Professional development for school improvement: Empowering learning communities.* Upper Saddle River, NJ: Prentice Hall.

Greenberg-Walt, C. L., & Robertson, A. G. (2001). The evolving role of executive leadership. In W. Bennis, G. M. Spreitzer, & T. G. Cummings (Eds.), *The future of leadership: Today's top leadership thinkers speak to tomorrow's leaders* (pp. 139-157). San Francisco, CA: Jossey-Bass.

Greenhalgh, T., & Wengraf, T. (2008). Collecting stories: Is it research? Is it good research? Preliminary guidance based on a Delphi study. *Medical Education, 42*, 242-247.

Griffin, R. W. (2008). *Fundamentals of management* (5th ed.). Boston, MA: Houghton Mifflin.

Gruber, H., & Mandl, H. (2001). Instructional psychology and the gifted. In K. A. Heller, F. J. Manks, R. Subotnik, & R. J. Sternberg, (Eds). *International handbook of giftedness and talents* (2nd ed.). New York, NY: Elsevier Science & Technology.

Guajardo, M. A. (2002). *Education for leadership development: Preparing a new generation of leaders* (Doctoral dissertation). Retrieved from ProQuest Dissertations and Theses database. (UMI No. 3099458)

Gunter, M. A., Estes, T. H., & Schwab, J. (2003). *Instruction: A models approach* (4th ed.). Upper Saddle River, NJ: Prentice Hall.

Halverson, P. K. (1999). Leadership skills and strategies for the integrated community health system. In R. W. Gilkey (Ed.), *The 21st century health care leader* (pp. 120-125). San Francisco, CA: Emory University School of Medicine.

Hancook, J. (2005). Why humanist communities should embrace charter schools. *Humanist, 65*(5), 38-39.

Handoussa, H. (2011, February). *What is after Egypt's youth revolution?* Retrieved from http://www.thedailynewsegypt.com/letters/what-after-egypts-youth-revolution.html

Hannum, M., Martineau, J. W., & Reinelt, C. (Eds.). (2007). *The handbook of leadership development evaluation.* San Francisco, CA: Jossey-Bass.

Hargens, L. (2001). Sampling procedures. In *Encyclopedia of sociology* (Vol. 4, pp. 2444-2449). New York, NY: Macmillan.

Hargreaves, E. (1997). The diploma disease in Egypt: Learning, teaching, and the monster of the secondary leaving certificate. *Assessment in Education: Principles, Policy & Practice, 4*, 161-177.

Haselden, P. G., & Algozzine, B. (2003). Use of affinity diagrams as instructional tools in inclusive classrooms. *Preventing School Failure, 47*(4), 187-189.

Harrison, B. (1999). The nature of leadership: Historical perspectives & the future. *Journal of California Law Enforcement, 33*, 24-34.

Hayes, J., Allinson, C. W., & Armstrong, S. J. (2004). Intuition, women managers and gendered stereotypes. *Personnel Review, 33*, 403-417.

Headington, E. W. (2001). Seeking a newer world. In W. Bennis, G. M. Spreitzer, & T. G. Cummings (Eds.), *The future of leadership: Today's top leadership thinkers speak to tomorrow's leaders* (pp. 226-240). San Francisco, CA: Jossey-Bass.

Healy, M., & Perry, C. (2000). Comprehensive criteria to judge validity and reliability of qualitative research within the realism paradigm. *Qualitative Market Research, 3*(3), 118-126.

Heckathorn, D. D. (2002). Respondent-driven sampling II: Deriving valid estimates from chain-referral samples of hidden populations. *Social Problems, 49,* 11-34. Retrieved from http://www.respondentdrivensampling.org/

Heifetz, R. A., & Laurie, D. L. (2003). The work of leadership. In J. M. Kouzes (Ed.), *Business leadership: A Jossey Bass reader* (pp. 543-567). San Francisco, CA: Jossey-Bass.

Helal, A., Ismail, M., & Gomaa, S. (2000). *Youth policies: Aspirations and challenges.* Cairo, Egypt: Public Administration Research and Consultation Center. Retrieved from http://www.parcegypt.org/english/link.php?cat_id=32&Id=396

Henderson, K. A., Whitaker, L. S., Bialeschki, M. D., Scanlin, M. M., & Thurber, C. (2007). Summer camp experiences: Parental perceptions of youth development outcomes. *Journal of Family Issues, 28,* 987-1007.

Hennessy, D., & Hicks, C. (2001). *The ideal attributes of chief nurses in Europe: A Delphi study for WHO: Europe.* Retrieved from http://www.euro.who.int /document/e74525.pdf

Herzog, E. (2007). *Future leaders.* Pacific Palisades, CA: Quest Consulting & Training.

Hoepfl, M. C. (1997). Choosing qualitative research: A primer for technology education researchers. *Journal of Technology Education, 9*(1), 47-63. Retrieved from http://scholar.lib.vt.edu/ejournals/JTE/v9n1/pdf/hoepfl.pdf

Hoffman, T. (1999). The meanings of competency. *Journal of European Industrial Training, 23*(6), 275-286. doi:10.1108/03090599910284650

Hopkins, N., & Saad, R. (2004). *Upper Egypt.* Cairo, Egypt: The American University in Cairo Press.

Horstmeier, R. P., & Ricketts, K. G. (2009). Youth leadership development through school-based civic engagement activities: A case study. *Journal of Leadership Education, 8,* 238-253. Retrieved from http://www.fhsu.edu/jole/issues /JOLE_8_2.pdf

House, R. J. (1996). Path-goal theory of leadership: Lessons, legacy, and a reformulated theory. *The Leadership Quarterly, 7,* 323-352.

Howell, D. C. (2005). Internal validity. In B. S. Everitt & D. C. Howell (Eds.), *Encyclopedia of statistics in behavioral science* (Vol. 2, pp. 936-937). West Sussex, England: Wiley.

Hsu, C., & Sanford, B. (2007a). The Delphi technique: Making sense of consensus. *Practical Assessment, Research & Evaluation, 12*(10). Retrieved from http://pareonline.net/pdf /v12n10.pdf

Hsu, C., & Sanford, B. (2007b). Minimizing non-response in the Delphi process: How to respond to non-response. *Practical Assessment Research & Evaluation, 12*(17). Retrieved from http://pareonline.net/getvn.asp?v=12&n=17

Huba, M. E., & Freed, J. E. (2000). *Learner-centered assessment on college campuses: Shifting the focus from teaching to learning.* New York, NY: Allyn & Bacon.

Huberman, A. M., & Miles, M. B. (2002). *The qualitative researcher's companion.* Thousand Oaks, CA: Sage.

Huebner, A., Walker, J., & McFarland, M. (2003). Staff development for the youth development professional: A critical framework for understanding the work. *Youth & Society, 33,* 204-225.

Hunt, O. (2007). *A mixed method design.* Retrieved from http://www.articlealley.com/article_185975_22.html

Huth, K. D. (2006). *Leadership competencies for financial healthcare executives in the U.S. Air Force* (Doctoral dissertation). Available from ProQuest Dissertations and Theses database. (UMI No. 3209247)

Ibrahim, B., Sallam S., El Tawila, S., El Gibaly, O., El Sahn, F., Lee, S. M., & Galal, O. (1999). *Transitions to adulthood: A national survey of Egyptian adolescents.* New York, NY: Population Council.

iEARN. (2010). *Home.* Retrieved from http://www.iearn.org/

Institute of International Education. (2009). *What is the student leadership discovery program?* Retrieved from http://www.iiemena-discovery.org/

International Development Research Center. (2009). *Module 10A: Overview of data collection techniques*. Retrieved from http://www.idrc.ca/en/ev-56606-201-1-DO_TOPIC.html

International Institute of Social Studies. (2009). *Children and youth studies: 2004-2007: Research on new and emerging needs of children and youth (NEN 2 and 3)*.Retrieved from http://www.iss.nl/layout/set/print/Children-and-Youth-Studies/Research

International Youth Foundation. (2007). *Education and employment alliance*. Retrieved from http://www.iyfnet.org/program/1265

International Youth Network. (2006). *Culture: The language of peace youth summer camps*. Retrieved from http://www.womenforpeaceinternational.org

Internet World Stats. (2009). *Egypt: Internet usage and telecommunications reports*. Retrieved from http://www.internetworldstats.com/af/eg.htm

INJAZ. (2010). *Our work*. Retrieved from http://www.injaz-egypt.org/en/work.html

Iqbal, S., & Pipon-Young, L. (2009). The Delphi method. *Psychologist, 22*, 598-600.

IREX. (2010). *Young women's leadership program*. Retrieved from http://www.irex.org

Jazzar, M., & Algozzine, B. (2006). *Critical issues in educational leadership*. Upper Saddle River, NJ: Prentice Hall/Pearson.

Jennings, L. B., Parra-Medina, D. M., Messias, D. K., & McLoughlin, K. (2006). Toward a critical social theory of youth empowerment. *Journal of Community Practice, 14*, 31-55.

Johnson, B., & Christensen, L. (2002). *Research and ethics in e-education*. Boston, MA: Pearson Custom Publishing.

Jonassen, D. H. (2006). A constructivist's perspective on functional contextualism. *Educational Technology, Research and Development, 54*, 43-48.

Kaplan, R. E., & Kaiser, R. B. (2003). Rethinking a classic distinction in leadership implications for the assessment and development of executives. *Consulting Psychology Journal: Practice & Research, 55,* 15-26.

Kark, R. (2004). The transformational leader: Who is (s)he? A feminist perspective. *Journal of Organizational Change Management, 17,* 160-176.

Kasim, K., & Shah, P. (2008). *Sustainability revisited: IT clubs in Egypt.* Retrieved from http://css.escwa.org.lb/ictd/17-19DEC08/d1.pdf

Keil, M., Tiwana, A., & Bush, A. (2002). Reconciling user and project manager perceptions of IT project risk: A Delphi study. *Information Systems Journal, 12,* 103-119.

Kennedy, H. P. (2004). Enhancing Delphi research: Methods and results. *Journal of Advanced Nursing, 45,* 504-511.

Khalil, N. (2002). The forgotten president. *Al Ahram Weekly, 595.* Retrieved from http://weekly.ahram.org.eg/2002/595/sc6.htm

Klau, M. (2006). Exploring youth leadership in theory and practice. *New Direction for Youth Development, 109,* 57-87.

Klenke, K. (2002). Cinderella stories of women leaders: Connecting leadership contexts and competencies. *Journal of Leadership and Organizational Studies, 9*(2),18-28.doi:10.1177/107179190200900202

Koenig, M. (2008). *Premises for successful leadership: How culture influence leaders.* Frankfurt, Germany: European University Viardina. Retrieved from http://books.google.com/books?id=z04yBSf1tgYC

Koinonia House. (2009). *Egypt's looming leadership crises.* Retrieved from http://www.khouse.org/enews_article/2008/1383/

Kouzes, J. M., & Posner, B. Z. (2002). *The leadership challenge* (3rd ed.). San Francisco, CA: Jossey-Bass.

Kress, C. (2006) Youth leadership and youth development: Connections and questions. *New Directions for Youth Development, 109,* 45-56.

Krishnan, V. R. (2001). Value systems of transformational leaders. *Leadership & Organization Development Journal, 22*(3), 126-132.

Krupp, S., & O'Neill, C. (2007). *What the future demands: The growing challenge of global leadership development.* Boston, MA: Harvard Business School.

Larson, R., & Farber, B. (2003). *Elementary statistics: Picturing the world* (2nd ed.). Upper Saddle River, NJ: Prentice-Hall.

Leap Africa. (2009). *Youth programmes.* Retrieved from http://www.leapafrica.org /Youth%20Leadership%20Programme.asp

Learning Theories Knowledgebase. (2009). *Social learning theory (Bandura).* Retrieved from http://www.learning-theories.com/social-learning-theory-bandura.html

Leedy, P. D., & Ormrod, J. E. (2001). *Practical research: Planning and design* (7th ed.). Upper Saddle River, NJ: Prentice/Hall.

Lerner, R. M., Lerner, J. V., Almerigi, J. B., Theokas, C., Phelps, E., & Gestsdottir, S. (2005). Positive youth development, participation in community youth development programs, and community contributions of fifth-grade adolescents: Findings from the first wave of the 4-H study of positive youth development. *Journal of Early Adolescence, 25,* 17-71.Retrieved from http://jea.sagepub.com/cgi/reprint/25/1/17

Lerner, R. M., Noh, E. R., & Wilson, C. (1998). *The parenting of adolescents and adolescents as parents: A developmental contextual perspective.* Retrieved from http://parenthood.library.wisc.edu/Lerner/Lerner.html

Leskiw, S., & Singh, P. (2007). Leadership development: Learning from best practices. *Leadership & Organization Development Journal, 28,* 444-464.

Libby, M., Sedonaen, M., & Bliss, S. (2006). The mystery of youth leadership development: The path to just communities. *New Directions for Youth Development, 109,* 13-25.

Lincoln, Y. S., & Guba, E. G. (1985). *Naturalistic inquiry.* Beverly Hills, CA: Sage.

Linstone, H. A., &Turoff, M. (2002). *The Delphi method: Techniques and applications.* Retrieved from http://www.is.njit.edu/pubs/delphibook/

Macdonald, J. E. (2003). *An exploration of the use of an online delphi method within an advocacy group* (Doctoral dissertation). Available from ProQuest Dissertations and Theses database. (UMI No. 305244882)

Mack, N., Woodsong, C., MacQueen, K., Guest, G., & Namey, E. (2009). *Qualitative research methods: A data collector's field guide.* Retrieved from http://www.fhi.org/NR/rdonlyres/etl7vogszehu5s4stpzb3 tyqlpp7rojv4waq37elpbyei3tgmc4ty6dunbccfzxtaj2rvbaubzmz4f/overvi ew1.pdf

MacNeil, C. A. (2006). Bridging generations: Applying "adult" leadership theories to youth leadership development. *New Direction for Youth development, 109,* 27-43.

Malcolm, C., Knighting, K., Forbat, L., & Kearney, N. (2009). Prioritisation of future research topics for children's hospice care by its key stakeholders: A Delphi study. *Palliative Medicine, 23,* 398-405.

Manca, D., Varnhagen, S., Brett-Maclean, P., Allan, G. M., & Szafran, O. (2008). Respect from specialists: Concerns of family physicians. *Canadian Family Physicians, 54,* 1434-1435.

Maner, M. (2000). *The research process: A complete guide and reference for writers.* New York, NY: McGraw-Hill.

Marczyk, G., DeMatteo, D., & Festinger, D. (2005). *Essentials of research design and*
    methodology. Hoboken, NJ: Wiley.

Margolis, H., & McCabe, P. P. (2006). Improving self-efficacy and motivation: What to do, what to say. *Intervention in School and Clinic, 41*(4), 218-228.

Marsh, C. J., & Willis, G. (2003). *Curriculum: Alternative approaches, ongoing issues* (3rd ed.). Upper Saddle River, NJ: Pearson.

Martin, A. J. (2003). The student motivation scale: Further testing of an instrument that measures school students' motivation. *Australian Journal of Education, 47,* 88-107.

Martin, J. (1991). *Experts' consensus concerning the content for an intercultural business communication course* (Doctoral dissertation).

Available from ProQuest Dissertations and Theses database. (UMI No. 9214866)

Masberg, B. A., Chase, D. M., & Madlem, M. S. (2003). A Delphi study of tourism training and education needs in Washington state. *Journal of Human Resources in Hospitatlity & Tourism, 2*(2), 1-21.

Mawsdley, R. D. (2002). Values orientation in American public schools. *Education and the Law, 14*, 77-82.

Maxwell, J. A. (2002). Understanding and validity in qualitative research. In M. A. Huberman & M. B. Miles (Eds.), *The qualitative researcher's companion* (pp. 37-63). Newbury Park, CA: Sage.

Maxwell, J. A. (2006). *Qualitative research design: An interactive approach* (2nd ed.). Newbury Park, CA: Sage.

McMillan, J. H., & Schumacher, S. (2006). *Research in education: Evidence-based inquiry* (6th ed.). Boston, MA: Prentice Hall.

Messinger, R. H. (2008). *Leadership competencies for effective global innovation teams* (Doctoral dissertation). Retrieved from ProQuest Dissertations and Theses database. (UMI No. 3326217)

Michie, J. (Ed.). (2001). *Reader's guide to the social sciences*. Chicago, IL: Fitzroy Dearborn.

Middle East Institute. (2008). *Educational reform in Egypt and the Arab world*. Retrieved from http://www.mideast.org/summary/educational-reform-egypt-and-arab-world

Middle East Youth Initiative. (2008). *Facts about Middle East youth*. Retrieved from http://www.shababinclusion.org

Mihyo, P. B., & Ogbu, O. (2000). *African youth on the information highway: Participation and leadership in community development*. Retrieved from http://www.idrc.ca/en/ev-9408-201-1-DO_TOPIC.html

Miller, D. C., & Salkind, N. J. (2002). *Handbook of research design and social measurement* (6th ed.). Newbury Park, CA: Sage.

Miller, J. (2008). *Standards for leadership knowledge, skills and values*. Retrieved from http://www.youthleadership.com/CYLN/Draft%20leadership%20standards%2004-15-2008.pdf

Mills, G. E. (2003). *Introduction to education research.* Upper Saddle River, NJ: Prentice Hall.

Mills, M. B., & Huberman, A. M. (1994). *Qualitative data analysis: A sourcebook of new methods* (2nd ed.). Thousand Oaks, CA: Sage.

Ministry of Education. (2010). *Partnerships.* Retrieved from http://www.emoe.org/

Minor, M. (2007). A community coalition prevention program: The long-term effects on *youths' self-esteem and illegal substance use* (Doctoral dissertation). Available from ProQuest Dissertations and Theses database. (UMI No. 3313179)

Mirza, S. K. (2002). Why critical scrutiny of Islam is an utmost necessity: Can reason blunt fanaticism? *Free Inquiry, 22*(2), 45-46. Retrieved from http://www.secularhumanism.org/index.php?section=library&page=mir za_22_2

Mitra, D. L. (2005). Adults advising youth: Leading while getting out of the way. *Educational Administration Quarterly, 41*, 520-553.Retrieved from http://eaq.sagepub.com/cgi/content/abstract/41/3/520

Morse, J., Barrett, M., Mayan, M., Olson, K., & Spiers, J. (2002). Verification strategies

for establishing reliability and validity in qualitative research. *International Journal of Qualitative Methods,1*(2). Retrieved fromhttp://www.ualberta.ca/~iiqm/backissues/1_2Final/pdf/morseetal.p df

Myers, M. (2000). Qualitative research and the generalizability question: Standing firm with Proteus. *The Qualitative Report, 4*(3/4). Retrieved from http://www.nova.edu/ssss/QR/QR4-3/myers.html

The National Democratic Party. (2009). *National youth policy.* Retrieved from http://www.ndp.org.eg/en/Policies/NationalYouthPolicy.aspx

Neuman, W. L. (2003). *Social research methods: Qualitative and quantitative approaches.* Upper Saddle River, NJ: Prentice Hall.

Northouse, P. G. (2010). *Leadership: Theory and practice* (5th ed.). Thousands Oaks, CA: Sage.

Okoli, C., & Pawlowski, S. (2004). The Delphi method as a research tool: An example design considerations and applications. *Information & Management, 42*, 15-29.

Organisation for Economic Co-operation and Development. (2005). *The definition and selection of key competencies: Executive summary.* Retrieved from http://www.oecd.org/dataoecd/47/61/35070367.pdf

Ornstein, A. C. (1997). How teachers plan lessons. *High School Journal, 80*, 227-237.

Owens, C., Ley, A., & Aiten, P. (2008). Do different stakeholder groups share mental health research priorities? A four-arm Delphi study. *Health Expectations, 11*, 418-431.

Oyserman, D. (2001). Self-concept and identity. In A. Tesser & N. Schwarz (Eds.), *Blackwell handbook of social psychology: Intraindividual processes* (pp. 22-43). Oxford, England: Blackwell.

Palys, T. (2008). Purposive sampling. In L. M. Given (Ed.), *The Sage encyclopedia of qualitative research methods* (Vol. 2, pp. 697-698). Thousand Oaks, CA: Sage.

Park, D. (1997). Androgynous leadership style: An integration rather than a polarization. *Leadership & Organization Development Journal, 18*(3), 166-171.

Patton, M. Q. (2002). *Qualitative research and evaluation methods* (3rd ed.). Thousand Oaks, CA: Sage.

Pearce, C. L., Sims H. P., Jr., Cox, J. F., Ball, G., Schnell, E., Smith, K. A., & Trevino, L. (2003). Transactors, transformers and beyond: A multi-method development of a theoretical typology of leadership. *The Journal of Management Development, 22*, 273-308. doi:10.1108/02621710310467587

Pelletier, J., & Corter, C. (2006). Integration, innovation, and evaluation in school-based. In B. Spodek & O. N. Saracho (Eds.), *Handbook of research on the education of young children* (2nd ed., pp. 477-496). New York, NY: Routledge.

Pittman, K. J., & Wright, M. (1991). *Bridging the gap: A rationale for enhancing the role of community organizations in promoting youth development*. Washington, DC: Academy for Educational Development.

Policy Project. (2005). Egypt: Youth champions working for policy implementation. *Youth Reproductive Health Policy, 4*. Retrieved from http://www.policyproject.com/pubs/YRHCBS/Egypt%20country%20brief.pdf

Powell, R. (2006). Evaluation research: An overview. *Library Trends, 55*, 102.

Prince, M., & Felder, R. (2006). Inductive teaching and learning methods: Definitions, comparisons, and research bases. *Journal of Engineering Education, 95*, 123-138.

Raley, G. (2005, August). *Qualitative quality: Criteria for evaluating ethnographic accounts*. Paper presented at the annual meeting of the American Sociological Association, Philadelphia, PA. Retrieved from http://www.allacademic.com/meta/p20711_index.html

Rea, L. M., & Parker, R. A. (2005). *Designing and conducting survey research: A comprehensive guide* (3rd ed.). San Francisco, CA: Jossey-Bass.

Reeder, H. M. (2005). Exploring male-female communication: Three lessons on gender. *The Journal of School Health, 75*(3), 115-118.

Reeves, A. (2005). Emotional intelligence: Recognizing and regulating emotions. *AAOHN Journal, 53*(4), 172-176.

Rice, K. (2009). Priorities in K-12 distance education: A Delphi study examining multiple perspectives research. *Journal of Educational Technology & Society, 12*(3), 163-177.

Ricketts, J. C., & Rudd, R. D. (2002). A comprehensive leadership education model to train, teach, and develop leadership in youth. *Journal of Career and Technical Education, 19*. Retrieved from http://scholar.lib.vt.edu/ejournals/JCTE/v19n1/ricketts.html

Rissel, C. (1994).Empowerment: The holy grail of health promotion? *Health Promotion International, 9*, 39-47.

Rodman, S. (2007). Educating youth for change. *International Journal of Diversity in Organisations, Communities & Nations*, 6(4), 95-100.

Rogers, J. L., & Shriberg, A. (2002). Leadership for the twenty-first century. In A. Shriberg, D. Shriberg, & C. Lloyd (Eds.), *Practicing leadership: Principles and applications* (2nd ed., pp. 206-230). New York, NY: Wiley.

Rogers, R. W., & Wellins, R. S. (2010). *Leadership beliefs*. Retrieved from http://www.ddiworld.com/pdf/ddi_leadershipbeliefs_wp.pdf

Rose, H. A. (2006). Asset-based development for child and youth care. *Reclaiming Children and Youth, 14*(4), 236-240.

Ross, J. L., & Schulz, R. A. (1999). Using the World Wide Web to accommodate diverse learning styles. *College Teaching, 47*(4), 123-130.

Rotary International. (2009). *Rotary youth leadership award*. Retrieved from http://www.rotary.org/en/studentsandyouth/youthprograms/RotaryYout hLeadershipAwards(RYLA)/Pages/ridefault.aspx

Routi, P. (2007). *Sampling*. Retrieved from http://www.uiah.fi/projekti/metodi/152.htm

Ruszkiewicz, J., Walker, J. R., & Pemberton, M. A. (2006). *Bookmarks: A guide to research and writing* (3rd ed.). Boston, MA: Prentice Hall.

Russell, R. (2003). *A practical theology of servant leadership*. Retrieved from http://www.regentuniversityonline.com/acad/global/publications/sl_pro ceedings/2003/russell_practical_theology.pdf

Saad Eddin, I. (1996). Reform and frustration in Egypt. *Journal of Democracy, 7*(4), 125-135. Retrieved from http://muse.jhu.edu/login?uri=/journals /journal_of_democracy/v007/7.4ibrahim.html

Salkind, N. (2003). *Exploring research* (5th ed.). Upper Saddle River, NJ: Prentice Hall.

Saunders, J. T., III. (2002). *Leadership for students program: Through their eyes* (Doctoral dissertation). Available from ProQuest Dissertations and Theses database. (UMI No. 3071867)

Save the Children. (2010). *Egypt.* Retrieved from http://www.savethechildren.org/

Sayed, F. (2004, April). *Innovation in public administration: The case of Egypt.* Symposium conducted at the meeting of the UNDESA in the frame of the Programme for the Promotion of Exchange of Administrative Innovation between Europe and the Mediterranean Region, Florence, Italy. Retrieved from http://unpan1.un.org/intradoc/groups/public/documents/un/unpan01590 4.pdf

Schermerhorn, J. R. (2010). *Management* (11th ed.). New York, NY: Wiley.

Schofield, J. W. (2002). Increasing the generalizability of qualitative research. In M. A. Huberman & M. B. Miles (Eds.), *The qualitative researcher's companion* (pp. 171–203). Newbury Park, CA: Sage.

Schunk, D. H. (2004). *Learning theories: An educational perspective* (4th ed.). Englewood Cliffs, NJ: Prentice Hall.

Schuster, J. P. (1994). Transforming your leadership style. *Association Management, 46*, 39-44.

Seeds of Peace. (2009). *About Seeds of Peace: An international model for conflict resolution.* Retrieved fromhttp://www.seedsofpeace.org/about

Serageldin, I. (2006). *Education for peace.* Retrieved from http://www.serageldin.com

Shahin, A. I. & Wright, P. L. (2004). Leadership in the context of culture: An Egyptian perspective. *Leadership & Organization Development Journal, 8*, 499-511. doi:10.1108/01437730410556743

Shank, G. D. (2006). *Qualitative research: A personal skills approach* (2nd ed.). Englewood Cliffs, NJ: Prentice Hall.

Sheard, A. G., & Kakabadse, A. P. (2004). A process perspective on leadership and team development. *The Journal of Management Development, 23*, 7.

Shehata, D. (2008). *Youth activism in Egypt.* Retrieved from http://arab-reform.net/IMG/pdf/ARB.23_Dina_Shehata_ENG.pdf

Sheridan, E. (2005). *Intercultural leadership competencies for United States business leaders in the new millennium* (Doctoral dissertation).

Retrieved from ProQuest Dissertations and Theses database. (UMI No. 3172360)

Shokr, A. (2004). *Youth socialism institute: Egyptian experience in developing leaders (1963-1976)*. Beirut, Lebanon: Center for Arab Union Studies.

Shriberg, A., Barnhart, G., & Shriberg, D. (2002). Modern leadership theories. In A. Shriberg, D. Shriberg, & C. Lloyd (Eds.), *Practicing leadership: Principles and applications* (2nd ed., pp. 151-168). New York, NY: Wiley.

Simon, M. K., & Francis, B. J. (2004). *The dissertation cookbook: From soup to nuts a practical guide to start and complete your dissertation* (3rd ed.). Dubuque, IA: Kendall/Hunt.

Skulmoski, G., Hartman, F., & Krahn, J. (2007). The Delphi method for graduate research. *Journal of Information Technology Education, 6*, 1-21.

Slocum, N. (2005). *Participatory methods toolkit, a practitioner's manual: Delphi*. Retrieved from http://www.viwta.be/files/ToolkitDelphi.pdf

Sparre, S. L., & Petersen, M. J. (2007). Youth and social change in Jordan and Egypt. *International Institute for the Study of Islam in the Modern World, 20*. Retrieved from http://www.isim.nl/files/Review_20/Review_20-14.pdf

Spreitzer, G. M., & Quinn, R. E. (2003). *Business leadership: A Jossey Bass reader*. San Francisco, CA: Jossey-Bass.

Sproull, N. D. (2004). *Handbook of research methods: A guide for practitioners and students in the social sciences* (3rd ed.). Lanham, MD: The Scarecrow Press.

State University. (2009). *Egypt: Educational system—Overview*. Retrieved from http://education.stateuniversity.com/pages/411/Egypt-EDUCATIONAL-SYSTEM-OVERVIEW.html

Steinberg, P. (2004). *New approaches to casual analysis in policy research*. Paper prepared for the panel Multi-Methods in Qualitative Research, Annual Convention of the American Political Science Association, Chicago. Retrieved from http://www.asu.edu/clas/polisci/cqrm/APSA2004/Steinberg.pdf

Stevens, R., Wineburg, S., Herrenkohl, L. R., & Bell, P. (2005). Comparative understanding of school subjects: Past, present, and future. *Review of Educational Research, 75*, 125-158.

Stolper, E., Van Royen, P., Van de Wiel, M., Van Bokhoven, M. Houben, P., Van der Weijden, T., & Jan Dinant, G. (2009). Consensus on gut feelings in general practice. *BMC Family Practice, 10*(9), 66.

Students in Free Enterprise. (2009). *Overview.* Retrieved from http://www.sife.org/aboutsife/Pages/Overview.aspx

SurveyMonkey. (2008). *Privacy policy.* Retrieved from http://www.SurveyMonkey.com

Syed, A. M., Hjarnoe, L., & Aro, A. R. (2009). The Delphi technique in developing
international health policies: Experience from the SARSControl project. *Internet Journal of Health, 8*(2), 1-5.

The Suzanne Mubarak Women's International Peace Movement. (2010). *Latest news.* Retrieved from http://www.womenforpeaceinternational.org/English/Pages/default.aspx#

Taylor, S. J., Bogdan, R. C., & Walker, P. (2000). Qualitative research. In A. E. Kazdin (Ed.), *Encyclopedia of psychology* (2nd ed., Vol. 6, pp. 489-491). Washington, DC: American Psychological Association.

Theory Into Practice. (2009). *Explorations in learning & instruction: The theory into practice database.* Retrieved from http://tip.psychology.org/vygotsky.html

Toth, M. (1996). *An experimental approach in evaluating instructional strategies to teach critical thinking in freshman nursing students* (Doctoral dissertation). Available from ProQuest Dissertations and Theses database. (UMI No. 9701171)

Trochim, W. M. K. (2006). *Internal validity.* Retrieved from http://www.socialresearchmethods.net/kb/intval.php

Trofimov, Y. (2009, April 20). Egypt's Gamal Mubarak aims to underpin growth. *The Wall Street Journal.* Retrieved from http://online.wsj.com

Tsou, H. (2005). An effective food and beverage management internship model in Taiwan. *Digital Abstracts International*, *66*(03), 925. (UMI No. 3168543)

Tubbs, S. L., & Jablokow, K. (2009). Leadership development and adaption-innovation theory. *The Business Review, 13*, 53-60.

Tubbs, S. L., & Schulz, E. (2006). Exploring a taxonomy of global leadership competencies and meta-competencies. *Journal of American Academy of Business, 8*(2), 29-34.

Tucker, B. A., & Russell, R. F. (2004). The influence of the transformational leader. *Journal of Leadership & Organizational Studies, 10*(4), 103-112.

United Nations. (2004). *Making commitments matter: A toolkit to evaluate youth policy*. Retrieved from http://www.un.org/esa/socdev/unyin/documents/Flashtoolkit.pdf

United Nations Development Programme. (2003). *Perspectives on the Arab human development report 2003*. Cairo, Egypt: Al-Siyassa Al-Dawliya.

United Nations Development Programme. (2007). *Human development report: Egypt*. Retrieved from http://hdrstats.undp.org/countries/country_fact_sheets/cty_fs_EGY.html

United Nations Development Programme. (2009). *Human development report*. Retrieved from http://hdr.undp.org/docs/network/hdr_net/Jordan_NYS_Concept_Paper.pdf

United Nations Development Programme. (2010). *Egypt's human development report – Youth in Egypt: Building our future*. Retrieved from http://www.undp.org.eg/Default.aspx?tabid=227

United Nations Education, Social and Cultural Organization. (2006). *Decentralization of education in Egypt*. Retrieved from http://unesdoc.unesco.org/images/0014/001470/147086E.pdf

United Nations International Children's Emergency Fund. (2010). *Egypt: Statistics*. Retrieved from http://www.unicef.org/infobycountry/egypt_statistics.html

United Nations Volunteers. (2008). *Think twice and the FGM-free village: UN in Egypt.* Retrieved from http://egypt-unv.org/news/doc/think-twice-and-the.html

Urwick, L. F. (1970). Theory Z. *SAM Advanced Management Journal, 35*, 14-22.

Van Eeden, R., Cilliers, F., & van Deventer, V. (2008). Leadership styles and associated
personality traits: Support for the conceptualisation of transactional and transformational leadership. *South African Journal of Psychology, 38,* 253-267.

Van Linden, J. A., & Fertman, C. I. (1998). *Youth leadership: A guide to understanding leadership development in adolescents.* San Francisco, CA: Jossey-Bass.

Van Maanen, J. (1998). *Qualitative studies of organizations: The administrative science quarterly series in organizational theory and behavior.* Thousand Oaks, CA: Sage.

Viehland, D. (2007). Research applications of the Delphi method. *CIS Group Research Seminars.* Retrieved from http://www.massey.ac.nz/~hryu/Delphi%20Method.pdf

Vigilante, A. (2003). *Education needs to be the motor of Egypt's development. Perspectives on the Arab human development report 2003.* Cairo, Egypt: Al-Siyassa Al-Dawliya.

Vogt, W. P. (2007). *Quantitative research methods for professionals.* Needham Heights, MA: Allyn & Bacon.

Vrasidas, C., & Zembylas, M. (2004). Online professional development: Lessons from the field. *Education & Training, 46*(6/7), 326.

Weiskittel, P. (1999). The concept of leadership. *ANNA Journal, 26*, 467.

Wenzel, S. (2008). *The future of African American male students in special education: A Delphi study* (Doctoral dissertation). Available from ProQuest Dissertations and Theses database. (UMI No. 3291631)

Whited, J. E. (2007). *Identifying required skills for virtual team leaders: A Delphi method study* (Doctoral dissertation). Available from ProQuest Dissertations and Theses database. (UMI No. 3324084)

Whitmore, P. G. (2004). Behavioral, cognitive, or brain-based training? *Performance Improvement, 43*(4), 9-15.

Wholey, J. S., Hatry, H., & Newcomer, K. E. (2004). *Handbook of practical program evaluation* (2nd ed.). San Francisco, CA: Jossey-Bass.

Wiggins, G. P. (1999). *Assessing student performance: Exploring the purpose and limits of testing.* Hoboken, NJ: Wiley.

Wilkinson, L. (1999). Statistical methods in psychology journals: Guidelines and explanations. *American Psychologist, 54*, 594-604.

Wilson, L. H. (2006). *A grounded theory study to discover how life experiences influence leader competencies* (Doctoral dissertation). Available from ProQuest Dissertations and Theses database. (UMI No. 3243735)

Wittrock, M. C. (2010). Learning as a generative process. *Educational Psychologist, 45*, 40-45.

Women leaders more persuasive. (2005). *New Zealand Management, 52*(6), 4-6.

World Bank. (2007). *Mapping of organizations working with and for youth in Egypt.* Retrieved from http://siteresources.worldbank.org/INTEGYPT/Resources /Youth_Report.pdf

World Bank. (2008). *A world bank's regional education report places Egypt among the middle performers.* Retrieved from http://web.worldbank.org/

World Bank. (2010). *Egypt.* Retrieved from http://data.worldbank.org/country/egypt-arab-republic

Wren, D. A. (2004). *The evolution of management thought* (5th ed.). New York, NY: Wiley.

Wright, R., & Stein, M. (2005). Snowball sampling. In K. Kempf-Leonard (Ed.), *Encyclopedia of social measurement* (Vol. 3, pp. 495-500). Dallas: TX, Elsevier.

Yin, R. K. (2004). *Applications of case study research: Applied social research methods series* (4th ed.). Thousand Oaks, CA: Sage.

Yousuf, M. I. (2007). Using experts' opinions through Delphi technique. *Practical Assessment, Research & Evaluation, 12*(4), 1-8. Retrieved from http://pareonline.net/getvn.asp?v=12&n=4

Youth Leadership Development Foundation. (2009). *About the foundation.* Retrieved from http://www.yldf.org/about.php

Youth Leadership Initiative. (2007). *Meet our talented team.* Retrieved from http://www.yliegypt.com/aboutus.aspx

Youth Partnership. (2005). *Youth policy: Here and now!* Retrieved from http://youth-partnership.coe.int/export/sites/default/youth-partnership/documents/Publications/Euromed/YouthPolicyReport_EN.pdf

Zami, M. S., & Lee, A. (2009). A review of the Delphi technique: To understand the factors influencing adoption of stabilised earth construction in low cost urban housing. *The Built & Human Environment Review, 2,* 1-14. Retrieved from http://www.tbher.org/index.php/bher/article/viewFile/36/20

Zedan, S. H. (2007). Community youth mapping: Female youth voices through empowerment and workforce preparation. *New Directions for Youth Development, 2116*, 87-98.

Zhao, J. (2007). Research in business. In *Encyclopedia of business and finance* (2nd ed., Vol. 2, pp. 206-230). Bingley, United Kingdom: Emerald Group.

Zurlinden, A. (2005). *Strengthening the YMCA movement: Younger leaders.* Workshop discussion at the World Alliance of YMCAs 150th anniversary event, Mumbai, India. Retrieved from http://www.ymca.int/uploads/media /LR_presentation_final_ymca_02.pdf

Appendix A: Letter of Intent and Consent Form

Letter of Intent and Consent Form

Dear Prospective Participant:

My name is Dalia Khalil and I am a student at the University of Phoenix working on a doctorate in Educational Leadership. I am conducting a research study entitled, "Defining a Youth Leadership Pipeline for Egypt." The research study is a qualitative research study supported by quantitative data method with a modified Delphi design and will be used to explore, examine, and refine the leadership skills and competencies needed for young leaders in Egypt, to determine how to develop multiple youth development and leadership opportunities for youth at the age 15–24, and to establish necessary effective evaluative methods.

Your participation will involve completing three rounds of questionnaires, which will take approximately 10-15 minutes to complete. The study's expected duration is February – December 2011. In addition, I would ask that you nominate and forward this request to others who you believe would be interested to participate and fits the criteria of participating stakeholders as follows:

- **Educators:** Participants who are educators will be chosen based on the level of participation (voluntarily or task-based) in the development and implementation of youth leadership activities (e.g., students' councils). The sample will include educators serving youth (15–24 years old). The sample of educators can include teachers, professors, principals, and counselors.

- **Parents:** The research participants who are parents and have volunteered to serve on leadership-level positions related to the age group 15–24 (e.g., school boards and sports clubs), reared children or youth (15–24 years old), and encouraged their children or youth to join activities with a leadership focus (e.g., Scouts), whether in Egypt or abroad. One parent from per family will be welcomed to have a diversity of families represented in the study.

- **Youth:** The youth members will include emerging adults (ages 19–24). The youth panel members need to have participated in a leadership role during their high school years or college life in Egypt or abroad (e.g., president of an activity club). This group could include students at public or private educational institutes.

- **Employers:** The employer stakeholders can include representatives from different sectors of employers: nongovernmental organizations, the private sector, the public sector, multinational organizations, and small and medium enterprises. The employer category participants need to be either the owner or the chief executive of an organization known to be adopting policies and cultural environments encouraging empowerment and leadership among its entry-level positions.

- **Community Leaders:** The community leader members will be graduates of the Youth Socialism Institute in Egypt in the 1960s. Community leaders need to hold a voluntarily leadership position (e.g., board member) in a community-based organization promoting the development and implementation of activities with a focus on youth development and leadership for ages 15–24. Community leaders might include religious, political, social, and entrepreneurial representatives.

Your participation in this study is voluntary. If you choose not to participate or to withdraw from the study at any time, you can do so without penalty or loss of benefit to yourself. If you choose to withdraw from the study, please inform me in a written format so I can remove your electronic mail address from the listing for reminders, and suggest another expert who might be interested in joining the study. The results of the research study may be published but your identity will remain confidential and your name will not be disclosed to any outside party. The data will only be analyzed and published as group statistics. No individual response data will be revealed, and your privacy will be protected. The results of the research study may be published, but your name will not be used and your responses will be maintained in confidence.

In this research, there are no expected risks to you as a result of participating in this research study. Participation is not intended nor expected to cause any mental or physical challenge. There is no possibility of stress or psychological, social, physical, or legal risks that are greater than those ordinarily encountered in their daily life. The study does not include any performance of routine physical or psychological examinations or tests. Also all communication with subjects will be direct and clear and therefore there will be no deception or misleading.

Although there may be no direct benefit to you, the possible benefit of your
participation is the contribution to the study of leadership and a study that can be used on
a national level for the welfare of Egypt's youth and future. Being involved in this
research study, participants will benefit by fostering evolution of a youth leadership
pipeline for Egypt, strengthening opportunities for culturally attuned youth leadership
efforts, contributing to long-term economic development workers for Egypt. After the
completion of the study, you will be eligible to participate in conferences and professional development opportunities related to the study's theme.

If you have any questions concerning the research study, please call me at xxx-xxx-xxxx and xxxxxxxxxxxxx@email.phoenix.edu. To access the questionnaire, please go towww.xxx.com/xxx and use the password "doctor11." The questionnaire will be accessible from xx/xx/xx to xx/xx/xx.

As a participant in this study, you should understand the following:
1. You may decline to participate or withdraw from participation at any time without consequences.

2. Your identity will be kept confidential.
3. The researcher has thoroughly explained the parameters of the research study and all of your questions and concerns have been addressed.
4. You understand that the collected data will be anonymous.
5. Data will be stored in a secure and locked area. The data will be held for a period of three years, and then destroyed.
6. The research results will be used for publication.

"By signing this form, you acknowledge that you understand the nature of the study, none potential risks to you as a participant, and the means by which your identity will be kept confidential. Your signature on this form also indicates that you are 18 years old or older and that you give your permission to voluntarily serve as a participant in the study described."

Signature of the interviewee _____ Date

_____

Signature of the researcher _____ Date

_____

Appendix B: Initial Pilot Study Questions

Initial Pilot Study Questions
I. Demographic Data:
a. Age group:
☐ 19 – 28   ☐ 29 – 38   ☐ 39 – 48
☐ 49 – 58   ☐ Older

b. Gender:
☐ Female   ☐ Male

c. Governorate:
☐ Cairo   ☐ Giza   ☐ Helwan
☐ Sixth of October   ☐ Qualubia

d. Education:
☐ College Education   ☐ MA or MS
☐ Doctorate or PhD   ☐ Others (Please specify)…………………………..

e. Stakeholder Classification:
☐ Parent   ☐ Educator   ☐ Youth (19 – 24 years)
☐ Employer   ☐ Community Leader

II. Leadership Experiences
a. In your pre-university leadership opportunities, what skills and competencies did you possess that were most helpful (please list all that apply)?
……………………………………………………………………………
……………………………………………………………………………
……………………………………………………………………………
………………………………………………

b. During your university/adult leadership opportunities, what skills and competencies did you possess that were most helpful (please list all that apply)?

....

....

....

....

c. In your experience, what leadership competencies in other people have you observed to be the most important to develop (please list all that apply)?

....

....

....

....

d. In your opinion, in what ways, or in which type of opportunities can youth (ages 15-24) be taught leadership competencies?

....
....
....
....

e. In your opinion, how can leadership opportunities and programs for youth (ages 15-24) be effectively evaluated?

....
....
....
....

f. In your opinion, what other additional information related to youth leadership was not covered in the questionnaire?

....
....
....
....

Appendix C: Copy of Round 1 Questionnaire

Defining a Youth Leadership Pipeline for Egypt - Round 1

1. Demographic Data

This section will include basic information about: age, gender, governorate of residence, educational background, and stakeholder classification.

For the purpose of this study, stakeholders were classified as:
• Parents: Participants who are parents and have volunteered to serve on leadership-level positions related to the age group 15–24 (e.g., school boards and sports clubs), reared children or youth (15–24 years old), and encouraged their children or youth to join activities with a leadership focus (e.g., Scouts), whether in Egypt or abroad.

• Educators: Participants who are educators with a high level of participation (voluntarily or task-based) in the development and implementation of youth leadership activities (e.g., students' councils) serving youth (15–24 years old). Educators can include teachers, professors, principals, and counselors.

• Youth: Young adults (ages 19–24)and have participated in a leadership role during their high school years or college life in Egypt or abroad (e.g., president of an activity club). This group could include students at public or private educational institutes.

• Employers: The employer stakeholders can include representatives from different sectors of employers: nongovernmental organizations, the private sector, the public sector, multinational organizations, and small and medium enterprises. The employer category participants are either the owner or the chief executive of an organization known to be adopting policies and cultural environments encouraging empowerment and leadership among its entry-level positions.

• Community Leaders: The community leader members may be graduates of the Youth Socialism Institute in Egypt in the 1960s. Community leaders need to hold a voluntarily leadership position (e.g., board member) in a community-based organization promoting the development and implementation of activities with a focus on youth development and leadership for ages 15–24. Community leaders might include religious, political, social, and entrepreneurial representatives.

Choose your stakeholder classification according to the listed criteria.

1. Age Group

☐ 19 – 28   ☐ 29 – 38   ☐ 39 – 48   ☐ 49 – 58   ☐ Older

Other (please specify)

2. Gender

☐ Female   ☐ Male

3. Governorate

☐ Cairo   ☐ Giza   ☐ Helwan   ☐ Sixth of October   ☐ Qulyebya

4. Education

☐ College Education   ☐ MA or MS   ☐ Doctorate or PhD   ☐ Others

Other (please specify)

Defining a Youth Leadership Pipeline for Egypt - Round 1

5. Stakeholder Classification

☐ Parent ☐ Educator ☐ Youth (19 – 24 years) ☐ Employer ☐ Community Leader

2. Leadership Experiences

This section will reflect on your personal experiences prior and during your university/adult leadership opportunities.

You are also requested to:
- reflect on observed leadership competencies in others
- list the type of opportunities youth (ages 15-24) can be taught leadership competencies
- describe how can leadership opportunities and programs for youth (ages 15-24) be effectively evaluated
- present other additional information related to youth leadership that was not covered in the questionnaire

*1. In your pre-university leadership opportunities, what skills and competencies did you possess that were most helpful (please list all that apply)?

3.

*1. During your university/adult leadership opportunities, what skills and competencies did you possess that were most helpful (please list all that apply)?

4.

*1. In your experience, what leadership competencies in other people have you observed to be the most important to develop (please list all that apply)?

5.

*1. In your opinion, in what ways can youth (ages 15-24) be taught leadership competencies? Which type of opportunities can youth be provided with?

6.

Defining a Youth Leadership Pipeline for Egypt - Round 1

*1. In your opinion, how can leadership opportunities and programs for youth (ages 15-24) be effectively evaluated?

7.

1. In your opinion, what other additional information related to youth leadership was not covered in the questionnaire?

8. Thank you

Thank you for taking the time to participate in my research study. I appreciate taking the time to complete the first round of questionnaires.

After collecting the data and summarizing the responses of the first round of questionnaires, you will be contacted shortly for the second round of questionnaire.

Without your support and all of the other participants, this study would not be possible. If you have any questions or concerns, please feel free to contact me at xxxxxxxxxxxx@email.phoenix.edu or xxx x xxx xxxx.

Thank you!

Appendix D: Common Themes and Frequency From Round 1 Response

Common Themes and Frequency from Round 1 Responses

Research question	Theme	Sub theme	Educators	Parents	Youth (19-24)	Employers	Community Leaders
R1	Values	Family values		2		1	
		Ethics and integrity		2		2	
		Fairness, sympathy, and forgiveness		2	2		
		Accepting and respecting others	1	6			3
	Leadership	Taking initiative and leading projects			6	5	3
		Inspiring people to act	6	5	8	8	6
		Strategic thinking, planning, and organizing	4	1		9	1
		Adaptive		2	1	3	
		Resolving conflict			1		
		Leading by example		1	2		
		Self discovery	3	1	2		
		Vision	5	3	2	5	3
		Managing change				1	
	Technical	Information technology,	1		4		1

Knowledge and Skills	computer, and media skills			1		1
	Fundraising			1	1	2
	Scientific and research skills	4	2	2		1
	Debating and public speaking	2		6	5	1
				5	3	
	Multilingual					
	Advising, coaching, and training skills					
Personal traits and skills:	Energetic and active			1	2	
	Attractive and presentable	2	2			
	Charismatic		2			
	Professional and competent	1	3	1		
Physical Traits	Confidence and self-esteem	1	3	4	2	
Personality and emotions	Determination, perseverance, and hard-working	1	1	8	4	2
	Firm, disciplined, responsible, and credible	4	4	5	5	1
	Social, passionate, sensitive, and helpful	1	8	6	1	
	Optimistic, ambitious, and		6			2

	risk-taker	1	2	1	4	2
	Observant and self-reflective	1	6	3	2	5
	Independent	1				
	Objective, flexible, and patient	3	3	6	4	4
Skills	Holistic views	17	9	11	12	10
	Creativity, problem solving, and decision-making	3	1	4	2	4
	Presentation and communication skills	2	2	1	5	1
	Stress and time management			3	1	
	Analytical and critical thinking					
	Negotiation skills					
R2	Family Support — Emotional support	1		2		2
	Financial support		1			
	Education and training methodologies — Quality of formal education	8	3	8	4	2
	Hands on activities and interactive workshop	4		1	2	

	training	1			1	1
	Coaching and mentoring	1			2	3
	Research					
	Summer jobs and internships					
Education and training content	Leadership and skills development	1	3		2	3
	Knowledge and information	1	2	1	2	
			3			
	Human values and moral standards	1		2	1	
	Independence and responsibility				1	
	Global affairs					
Extra curricula activities	Simulations, dialogue, and debates	3	3		2	4
	Meetings, camps, and youth summits	2	2	1	2	5
	Field trips				1	
Community activities	Following a role model	1	1	2		
	Conducting social work and community service	3	4	3	5	3
	projects	1		3	3	2

	Volunteering at NGOs and charity organizations	3	5	3	1	2
National and international opportunitie s	Sports, clubs, and competitions	1	1	5	1	
	Virtual and physical exchange programs	1	1			3
	Travel, study abroad, and host family stays	2	5			1
	Civic engagement and political parties	1				1
Diversity	Participation in a diversity of activities	2	2	1	2	
	Exposure to a diversity of views				1	2
	Freedom of expression					
R3	Assessment tools	End of program's presentation or project	1	1	2	2	1
	Survey/interview participants to measure learning	3	1			
	Assessment centers	2		2	1	
	Pre/Post knowledge check	2	4	2	1	
	Assess learning through					

Category	Item					
	participants' interaction					2
	Journals/reflections/reports					1
	School/university expeditions and conferences					
Evaluation tools	360 Degree survey				2	1
	Feedback from participants and instructors/trainers			2	1	
	Survey				3	
	employers/employers' expectations				1	
	Focus group sessions				1	
	Success stories	2		1	2	
	Evaluation forms to measure satisfaction level		1			
	Monitoring		1			
	Mentoring and coaching			1		
	Evaluating program's content in comparison with other countries		2		2	
	Output based evaluation (measuring objectives through key performance		1			4

	indicators)					
	Qualitative and quantitative research				1	
Long term impact	Monitor progress over years e.g. career		1			
	Entrepreneurship		1			2
	Transformation of knowledge to others					1
	Personality changes	1		1		
	Sustainability					
	Community involvement and impact		1	1		
	Fast track and high flyers opportunities		1			

Appendix E: Round 1: Responses to Question 6

Round 1
Responses to question 6

Description	Response
Skipped question	9 participants
Responded with None	- NA - Nothing. I think it covered all the relevant points - Can't think of one now - None - Seemed pretty thorough - Nothing I can think of - No - Nothing that I am aware of as the questions are general enough to cover anything and everything - I think you covered all of them - I think nothing else - I believe they were all covered
Suggestions related to the questionnaire's layout	- I believe this questionnaire could have been more helpful if there were choices to make as it would provide ideas and then we could comment openly. I hope I could have helped but it is hard to respond when the objective is not really clear. Sorry - I was expecting the survey to offer a wider selection of multiple-choice kind of questions to prove the due-diligence effort exerted in the design phase rather than leaving blank spaces to the respondent. - I would suggest to list a set of competencies and we choose - You needed to give a definition for Leadership and to categorize it; i.e. in business or school

	administration etc. - Perhaps the leadership competencies, frameworks or models targeted/addressed in the study
Factors hindering youth leadership	- What hinders youth leadership - Factors currently spread in our culture and society that may hinder the development of such skills among the next generation
Different roles	- Role of school and families in nurturing leadership potentials in youth - Role of media - Who will provide these opportunities? depend if it's a local or international organization. There are pros and cons for each case that needs to be measured before taking offers from sponsors - Tackling the point regarding the role of the government/local community or active civil society in preparing youth leaders
Leadership	- Issues related to the own vision and mission might be very linked to youth leadership and some questions on that should give a clear and stable impression on the youth leadership. - Leadership should be defined as Responsibility and Duty. Only those who believe in this should undertake the training to guide others. There are different aspects of life that need guidance from cleanliness, hygiene to social integration, leaders should be rotated amongst the different regions each radiating his point as not all followers of one group will be guided by the same leader. Rotation allows flexibility and integration. - The Inspiration Leadership Traits. This is important for the people, particularly for the youth that want to be inspired. In fact, there is a

	whole class of people who will follow an inspiring leader–even when the leader has no other qualities. If you have developed the other traits, being inspiring is usually just a matter of communicating clearly and with passion. Being inspiring means telling people how your organization is going to change the world
Process of identifying leaders	- How to discover leaders at pre-university level? What can be done to promote leadership in youth? - How to deal with this problem
Evaluation	- The methodology of evaluating youth themselves not the programs only. It needs to include multiple choice questions rather than open-ended questions - Evaluating their leadership level before any training or awareness to classify them accordingly
Others	- Male/Female: social effects - Financial status

Appendix F: Copy of Round 2 Questionnaire

Round 2

Defining a Youth Leadership Pipeline for Egypt: A Delphi Study

Dear Expert Panelist,

Thank you again for your participation in the study, Defining a Youth Leadership Pipeline for Egypt: A Delphi Study. The next survey, which you can access on SurveyMonkey until November 4, 2011, is the second round of the Delphi study. All expert responses from the survey in Round 1 have been processed and are included in the survey for Round 2.

Round 2 is comprised of a multiple choice survey. You will be asked to rate the expert responses from Round 1 according to the following categories:
5- Very important, 4- Important, 3- Neutral, 2- Not very important, 1- Not important

You will be rating each of the responses according to your opinion on how the responses relate and contribute to the youth leadership development. Your identification and responses will be kept confidential, and no responses will be identified with any other person. I will be the only individual with access to the survey results.

This survey needs to be completed by November 4, 2011 by 11:00 pm. If you encounter any problems, or have questions or concerns, please contact xxxxx xxxxxx at xxxxxxxxxxxx@email.phoenix.edu or xxx x xxx xxxx. Thank you for your support in this study.

Sincerely,

Dalia Khalil
Doctoral Candidate, University of Phoenix

Competencies and Skills

In Round One, your responses contributed to the identification of four common themes of competencies and skills that can contribute most to the development of leadership in youth (age 15-24). The common themes are: values, leadership, technical knowledge and skills, and personal traits and skills. Under each common theme, there are a number of categories and subcategories that you will need to rate according to importance. The common themes are listed below in no particular order of frequency.
Based on your personal experiences and observations, please rate the themes according to the following scale:
5- Very important 4- Important 3- Neutral 2- Not very important 1- Not important

1. Values: How important are the following values (if possessed by youths) in contributing to youth leadership development?

	5- Very important	4- Important	3- Neutral	2- Not very important	1- Not important
a. Family values	☐	☐	☐	☐	☐
b. Ethics and integrity	☐	☐	☐	☐	☐
c. Fairness, sympathy, and forgiveness	☐	☐	☐	☐	☐
d. Accepting and respecting others	☐	☐	☐	☐	☐

Round 2

2. Leadership: How important are the following leaderships aspects (if possessed by youth) in contributing to youth leadership development?

	5- Very important	4- Important	3- Neutral	2- Not very important	1- Not important
a. Taking initiative and leading projects	☐	☐	☐	☐	☐
b. Inspiring people to act	☐	☐	☐	☐	☐
c. Strategic thinking, planning, and organizing	☐	☐	☐	☐	☐
d. Adaptive	☐	☐	☐	☐	☐
e. Resolving conflict	☐	☐	☐	☐	☐
f. Leading by example	☐	☐	☐	☐	☐
g. Self discovery	☐	☐	☐	☐	☐
h. Vision	☐	☐	☐	☐	☐
i. Managing change	☐	☐	☐	☐	☐

3. Technical knowledge and skills: How important are the following technical knowledge and skills (if possessed by youth) in contributing to youth leadership development?

	5- Very important	4- Important	3- Neutral	2- Not very important	1- Not important
a. Information technology, computer, and media skills	☐	☐	☐	☐	☐
b. Fundraising	☐	☐	☐	☐	☐
c. Scientific and research skills	☐	☐	☐	☐	☐
d. Debating and public speaking	☐	☐	☐	☐	☐
e. Multilingual	☐	☐	☐	☐	☐
f. Advising, coaching, and training skills	☐	☐	☐	☐	☐

4. Personal traits and skills: How important are the following physical traits (if possessed by youth) in contributing to youth leadership development?

	5- Very important	4- Important	3- Neutral	2- Not very important	1- Not important
a. Energetic and active	☐	☐	☐	☐	☐
b. Attractive and presentable	☐	☐	☐	☐	☐
c. Charismatic	☐	☐	☐	☐	☐
d. Professional and competent	☐	☐	☐	☐	☐

Round 2

5. Personal traits and skills: How important are the following personality and emotional aspects (if possessed by youth) in contributing to youth leadership development?

	5- Very important	4- Important	3- Neutral	2- Not very important	1- Not important
a. Confidence and self-esteem	☐	☐	☐	☐	☐
b. Determination, perseverance, and hard-working	☐	☐	☐	☐	☐
c. Firm, disciplined, responsible, and credible	☐	☐	☐	☐	☐
d. Social, passionate, sensitive, and helpful	☐	☐	☐	☐	☐
e. Optimistic, ambitious, and risk-taker	☐	☐	☐	☐	☐
f. Observant and self-reflective	☐	☐	☐	☐	☐
g. Independent	☐	☐	☐	☐	☐
h. Objective, flexible, and patient	☐	☐	☐	☐	☐
i. Holistic views	☐	☐	☐	☐	☐

6. Personal traits and skills: How important are the following skills (if possessed by youth) in contributing to youth leadership development?

	5- Very important	4- Important	3- Neutral	2- Not very important	1- Not important
a. Creativity, problem solving, and decision-making	☐	☐	☐	☐	☐
b. Presentation and communication skills	☐	☐	☐	☐	☐
c. Stress and time management	☐	☐	☐	☐	☐
d. Analytical and critical thinking	☐	☐	☐	☐	☐
e. Negotiation skills	☐	☐	☐	☐	☐

Environmental factors and type of leadership opportunities

In Round One, your responses contributed to the identification of four common themes of environmental factors and type of leadership opportunities that can contribute most to the teaching of leadership in youth (age 15-24). The common themes are: family support, education and training, activities, and diversity. Under each common theme, there are a number of categories and subcategories that you will need to rate according to importance. The common themes are listed below in no particular order of frequency. Based on your personal experiences and observations, please rate the themes according to the following scale:
5- Very important 4- Important 3- Neutral 2- Not very important 1- Not important

Round 2

7. How important are the following family support aspects in contributing to the teaching of leadership in youth (age 15-24)?

	5- Very important	4- Important	3- Neutral	2- Not very important	1- Not important
Emotional support	☐	☐	☐	☐	☐
Financial support	☐	☐	☐	☐	☐

8. How important are the following education and training methodologies in contributing to the teaching of leadership in youth (age 15-24)?

	5- Very important	4- Important	3- Neutral	2- Not very important	1- Not important
a. Quality of formal education	☐	☐	☐	☐	☐
b. Hands on activities and interactive workshop training	☐	☐	☐	☐	☐
c. Coaching and mentoring	☐	☐	☐	☐	☐
d. Research	☐	☐	☐	☐	☐
e. Summer jobs and internships	☐	☐	☐	☐	☐

9. How important are the following education and training content in contributing to the teaching of leadership in youth (age 15-24)?

	5- Very important	4- Important	3- Neutral	2- Not very important	1- Not important
a. Leadership and skills development	☐	☐	☐	☐	☐
b. Knowledge and information	☐	☐	☐	☐	☐
c. Human values and moral standards	☐	☐	☐	☐	☐
d. Independence and responsibility	☐	☐	☐	☐	☐
e. Global affairs	☐	☐	☐	☐	☐

10. How important are the following extra curricula activities in contributing to the teaching of leadership in youth (age 15-24)?

	5- Very important	4- Important	3- Neutral	2- Not very important	1- Not important
a. Simulations, dialogue, and debates	☐	☐	☐	☐	☐
b. Meetings, camps, and youth summits	☐	☐	☐	☐	☐
c. Field trips	☐	☐	☐	☐	☐

Round 2

11. How important are the following community activities in contributing to the teaching of leadership in youth (age 15-24)?

	5- Very important	4- Important	3- Neutral	2- Not very important	1- Not important
a. Following a role model	☐	☐	☐	☐	☐
b. Conducting social work and community service projects	☐	☐	☐	☐	☐
c. Volunteering at NGOs and charity organizations	☐	☐	☐	☐	☐

12. How important are the following national and international opportunities and activities in contributing to the teaching of leadership in youth (age 15-24)?

	5- Very important	4- Important	3- Neutral	2- Not very important	1- Not important
a. Sports, clubs, and competitions	☐	☐	☐	☐	☐
b. Virtual and physical exchange programs	☐	☐	☐	☐	☐
c. Travel, study abroad, and host family stays	☐	☐	☐	☐	☐
d. Civic engagement and political parties	☐	☐	☐	☐	☐

13. How important are the following diversity aspects in contributing to the teaching and development of leadership in youth (age 15-24)?

	5- Very important	4- Important	3- Neutral	2- Not very important	1- Not important
Participation in a diversity of activities	☐	☐	☐	☐	☐
Exposure to a diversity of views	☐	☐	☐	☐	☐
Freedom of expression	☐	☐	☐	☐	☐

Assessment, evaluation, and long term impact

In Round One, your responses contributed to the identification of three common themes of effective methods to evaluate youth leadership development in youth (age 15-24). The common themes are: assessment, evaluation, and long term impact. Under each common theme, there are a number of categories and subcategories that you will need to rate according to importance. The common themes are listed below in no particular order of frequency. Based on your personal experiences and observations, please rate the themes according to the following scale:
5- Very important 4- Important 3- Neutral 2- Not very important 1- Not important

Round 2

14. How important are the following assessment tools in contributing to the evaluation leadership development in youth (age 15-24)?

	5- Very important	4- Important	3- Neutral	2- Not very important	1- Not important
a. End of program's presentation or project	☐	☐	☐	☐	☐
b. Survey/interview participants to measure learning	☐	☐	☐	☐	☐
c. Assessment centers	☐	☐	☐	☐	☐
d. Pre/Post knowledge check	☐	☐	☐	☐	☐
e. Assess learning through participants' interaction	☐	☐	☐	☐	☐
f. Journals/reflections/reports	☐	☐	☐	☐	☐
g. School/university expeditions and conferences	☐	☐	☐	☐	☐

15. How important are the following evaluation tools in contributing to the evaluation leadership development in youth (age 15-24)?

	5- Very important	4- Important	3- Neutral	2- Not very important	1- Not important
a. 360 Degree survey	☐	☐	☐	☐	☐
b. Feedback from participants and instructors/trainers	☐	☐	☐	☐	☐
c. Survey employers/employers' expectations	☐	☐	☐	☐	☐
d. Focus group sessions	☐	☐	☐	☐	☐
e. Success stories	☐	☐	☐	☐	☐
f. Evaluation forms to measure satisfaction level	☐	☐	☐	☐	☐
g. Monitoring	☐	☐	☐	☐	☐
h. Mentoring and coaching	☐	☐	☐	☐	☐
i. Evaluating program's content in comparison with other countries	☐	☐	☐	☐	☐
j. Output based evaluation (measuring objectives through key performance indicators)	☐	☐	☐	☐	☐
k. Qualitative and quantitative research	☐	☐	☐	☐	☐

Round 2

16. How important are the following long term impact tools in contributing to the evaluation leadership development in youth (age 15-24)?

	5- Very important	4- Important	3- Neutral	2- Not very important	1- Not important
a. Monitor progress over years e.g. career	☐	☐	☐	☐	☐
b. Entrepreneurship	☐	☐	☐	☐	☐
c. Transformation of knowledge to others	☐	☐	☐	☐	☐
d. Personality changes	☐	☐	☐	☐	☐
e. Sustainability	☐	☐	☐	☐	☐
f. Community involvement and impact	☐	☐	☐	☐	☐
g. Fast track and high flyers opportunities	☐	☐	☐	☐	☐

Hindering factors for youth leadership development

In round one, some of your comments highlighted the importance of identifying the hindering factors to develop youth leadership.

17. In your opinion, what are the hindering factors that may affect the development of youth leadership (age 15-24)?

Thank you

Thank you for your time and effort to support this study.

Appendix G: Results of Round 2

Theme	Subtheme	Very Important	Important	Neutral	Not Very Important	Not Important	Mean
Values	Family values	8	14	2	1	0	4.16
	Ethics and integrity	20	5	0	0	0	4.8
	Fairness, sympathy, and forgiveness	14	10	0	0	1	4.44
	Accepting and respecting others	22	3	0	0	0	4.88
Leadership	Taking initiative and leading projects	17	7	1	0	0	4.64
	Inspiring people to act	17	6	1	1	0	4.56
	Strategic thinking, planning, and organizing	15	9	1	0	0	4.56
	Adaptive	11	12	2	0	0	4.36
	Resolving conflict	14	10	1	0	0	4.52
	Leading by example	9	13	3	0	0	4.24
	Self discovery	11	10	3	0	0	4.24
	Vision	16	7	2	0	0	4.56
	Managing change	13	10	2	0	0	4.44
Technical Knowledge and Skills	Information technology, computer, and media skills	12	9	4	0	0	4.32
		2	12	9	1	0	3.52

Category	Item						Mean
	Fundraising	2	15	6	2	0	3.68
	Scientific and research skills	12	12	1	0	0	4.44
	Debating and public speaking	9	12	3	1	0	4.16
	Multilingual	10	12	2	1	0	4.24
	Advising, coaching, and training skills						
Physical Traits	Energetic and active	19	5	1	0	0	4.72
	Attractive and presentable	4	17	4	0	0	4.00
	Charismatic	9	13	3	0	0	4.24
	Professional and competent	19	6	0	0	0	4.76
Personality and Emotions		18	7	0	0	0	4.72
	Confidence and self-esteem	18	7	0	0	0	4.72
	Determination, perseverance, and hard-working	19	5	1	0	0	4.72
	Firm, disciplined, responsible, and credible	7	14	4	0	0	4.12
		9	16	1	0	0	4.48
	Social, passionate, sensitive, and helpful	12	12	1	0	0	4.44

Category	Item						Mean
Skills	Optimistic, ambitious, and risk-taker	12	10	3	0	0	4.36
	Observant and self-reflective	13	12	0	0	0	4.52
	Independent	8	10	5	2	0	3.96
	Objective, flexible, and patient	16	9	0	0	0	4.64
	Holistic views	14	11	0	0	0	4.56
	Creativity, problem solving, and decision-making	14	9	2	0	0	4.48
	Presentation and communication skills	10	14	1	0	0	4.36
	Stress and time management	11	11	3	0	0	4.32
	Analytical and critical thinking						
	Negotiation skills						
Family Support	Emotional support	11	12	2	0	0	4.36
	Financial support	3	12	6	2	2	3.48
Education and training	Quality of formal education	14	9	2	0	0	4.48
	Hands on activities and methodologie	13	10	2	0	0	4.44

Category	Item						Mean
s	interactive workshop	14	8	3	0	0	4.44
	training	6	12	6	0	1	3.88
	Coaching and mentoring	8	11	6	0	0	4.08
	Research						
	Summer jobs and internships						
Education and training content	Leadership and skills development	17	7	1	0	0	4.64
	Knowledge and information	8	12	5	0	0	4.12
	Human values and moral standards	11	12	2	0	0	4.36
	Independence and responsibility	16	8	1	0	0	4.6
	Global affairs	3	15	8	0	0	3.96
Extra curricula activities	Simulations, dialogue, and debates	14	8	3	0	0	4.44
	Meetings, camps, and youth summits	16	6	3	0	0	4.52
	Field trips	8	11	6	0	0	4.08
Community activities	Following a role model	9	10	5	1	0	4.08
	Conducting social work and community service	14	9	1	1	0	4.44

	projects	14	8	2	1	0	4.40
National and international opportunities	Volunteering at NGOs and charity organizations	4	14	7	0	0	3.88
	Sports, clubs, and competitions	11	13	1	0	0	4.4
	Virtual and physical exchange programs	12	10	4	0	0	4.48
	Travel, study abroad, and host family stays	8	10	5	2	0	3.96
	Civic engagement and political parties	10	10	4	1	0	4.16
Diversity	Participation in a diversity of activities	14	9	2	0	0	4.48
	Exposure to a diversity of views	11	13	1	0	0	4.48
	Freedom of expression	10	10	4	1	0	4.40
Assessment tools	End of program's presentation or project	5	13	6	1	0	4.16
	Survey/interview participants to measure learning	7	6	11	1	0	3.88
	Assessment centers	7	9	8	1	0	3.76
	Pre/Post knowledge	9	13	3	0	0	3.88

						Mean
check						
Assess learning through participants' interaction	5	8	10	1	1	3.60
Journals/reflections/reports	5	13	7	0	0	3.92
School/university expeditions and conferences						
Evaluation tools — 360 Degree survey	6	9	8	2	0	3.76
Feedback from participants and instructors/trainers	9	14	2	0	0	4.28
Survey	7	12	6	0	0	4.04
employers/employers' expectations	11	7	7	0	0	4.16
Focus group sessions	7	13	4	1	0	4.04
Success stories	4	10	6	5	0	3.52
Evaluation forms to measure satisfaction level	10	8	7	0	0	4.12
Monitoring	16	5	4	0	0	4.48
Mentoring and coaching	5	10	8	2	0	3.72
Evaluating program's content in comparison	10	12	2	1	0	4.24

	with other countries					
	Output based evaluation (measuring objectives through key performance indicators)	4	11	9	1	0	3.72
	Qualitative and quantitative research					
Long term impact	Monitor progress over years e.g. career	9	13	3	0	0	4.24
	Entrepreneurship	12	8	5	0	0	4.28
	Transformation of knowledge to others	13	8	4	0	0	4.36
	Personality changes	12	8	5	0	0	4.28
	Sustainability	13	8	5	0	0	4.48
	Community involvement and impact	11	10	3	1	0	4.24
	Fast track and high flyers opportunities	6	6	12	1	0	3.68

Appendix H: Round 2-Factors Hindering Youth Leadership Development

Round 2
Factors hindering youth leadership development

Themes	Repetition
Education and training	Lack of opportunities for learning, researching, training, and exposure (11)
	Lack of incentives, challenges, and career planning (2)
	Concentration on academic education only and insufficient channels to experience ability to lead (4)
Financial issues	Lack of funding and infrastructure required to develop leadership programs (5)
Social and cultural issues	Negative family influences, mindset of parents/adults not believing in youth leadership (6)
	Not being exposed to different environments, other cultures, and other people (3)
	Social barriers that enforce resistance to change hindering creativity, support for new ideas, , and practice of leadership in life

	situations (3) Absence of a role model (2)
Support and mentoring	Lack of skilled and knowledgeable trainers to discover leadership talents, offer support and mentoring, and provide feedback and guidance (5)
Others	

Answered question   21
Skipped question   4

Appendix I: Copy of Round 3 Questionnaire

Round 3

Defining a Youth Leadership Pipeline for Egypt: A Delphi Study (Round 3)

Dear Participant,

Thank you for participating in the first and second rounds of the study Defining a Youth Leadership Pipeline for Egypt: A Delphi Study. The goal of the Delphi study is to establish a consensus among participating experts on the leadership competencies, leadership opportunities and programs, and evaluative tools necessary for future programs promoting youth leadership (age 15-24).
The Delphi survey design is comprised of three rounds to complete the study.

The third round is your last chance to give your feedback and agreement about the data provided in Round 2 of the study. This round focuses on strengthening the consensus from the second round data. A consensus for each question was determined when 80% or more of the panelists were in agreement which is represented by a weighted mean rating equivalent or higher than a rating of 4.0.

As an expert panelists and research participant in this study, you will determine if the questions that met consensus in Round 2 can contribute to youth leadership development. You can also submit your feedback (if needed) to any of the themes listed. You will also be ranking the responses according to your opinion on how the responses relate and contribute to the youth leadership development.

Your identification and responses will be kept confidential, and no responses will be identified with any other person. I will be the only individual with access to the survey results.

This survey needs to be completed by December 24, 2011 by 11:00 pm. If you encounter any problems, or have questions or concerns, please contact xxxxx xxxxxx at xxxxxxxxxxxx@email.phoenix.edu or xxx x xxx xxxx.
Thank you for your support in this study.

Sincerely,
Dalia Khalil
Doctoral Candidate, University of Phoenix

Round 3

*1. The following aspects/factors were identified as essential capabilities, skills, and competencies contributing to youth leadership development in responses from Round One and received the highest mean value in Round 2. Please rank them in the order that best express your opinion as contributors to youth leadership development (1=First; 6= Sixth). Please only assign one rank per item. Items are listed according to alphabetical order.

Rank the order you would choose to the below items in terms of contribution to youth leadership development.

	First	Second	Third	Fourth	Fifth	Sixth
Leadership	○	○	○	○	○	○
Personality and emotions	○	○	○	○	○	○
Physical traits	○	○	○	○	○	○
Skills	○	○	○	○	○	○
Technical knowledge and skills	○	○	○	○	○	○
Values	○	○	○	○	○	○

Comments

Round 3

*2. The following aspects/factors were identified as activities and opportunities contributing to teaching youth leadership development in responses from Round One and received the highest mean value in Round 2. Please rank them in the order that best express your opinion as contributors to teaching youth leadership development (1=First; 6= Sixth). Please only assign one rank per item. Items are listed according to alphabetical order.

Rank the order you would choose to the below items in terms of contribution to the teaching of youth leadership development.

	First	Second	Third	Fourth	Fifth	Sixth
Community activities	○	○	○	○	○	○
Diversity aspects	○	○	○	○	○	○
Education and training content	○	○	○	○	○	○
Education and training methodologies	○	○	○	○	○	○
Extra curicula activities	○	○	○	○	○	○
National and international opportunities and activities	○	○	○	○	○	○

Comments

*3. The following aspects/factors were identified as procedures contributing to the evaluation process of youth leadership development in responses from Round One and received the highest mean value in Round 2. Please rank them in the order that best express your opinion as contributors to evaluating youth leadership development (1=First; 2= Second). Please only assign one rank per item. Items are listed according to alphabetical order.

Rank the order you would choose to the below items in terms of contribution to the evaluation of youth leadership development.

	First	Second
Using evaluation tools	○	○
Measuring long term impact	○	○

Comments

Round 3

✱ 4. In Round 2, a significant number of experts listed multiple factors hindering youth leadership development. What are your recommendations to overcome the following four factors hindering youth leadership development for ages (15-24) in Egypt?

a. Lack of opportunities for learning, researching, training, and exposure

b. Lack of funding and infrastructure required to develop leadership programs

c. Negative family influences, mindset of parents/adults not believing in youth leadership

d. Lack of skilled and knowledgeable trainers/coaches/counselors to discover leadership talents, offer support and mentoring, and provide feedback and guidance

Appendix J: Round 3 Participants' Recommendations

Round 3
Participants' Recommendations

a. Lack of opportunities for learning, researching, training, and exposure

Sequence	Stakeholder	Suggestions
2	CL6	Introduce more activities, researches, training and exposures in programs, especially in national programs, as well as more extra-curricular and community activities
3	P7	This can be done through the creation of programs with the different chambers of commerce
4	Edu1	Build small local community educational centers with libraries as main feature and free correspondence courses
5	Y3	Targeted programs at schools
6	Edu4	Activate online education
7	E1	Encouraging students to take part in extracurricular activities on school campus and inform them about the ones outside
8	P2	Available advanced research tools, enable apprenticeship degrees rather than academic degrees, encourage international training exchange
10	P1	Make the youth aware of the importance of these issues early on in school life and show institutions the various benefits of the youth being granted such opportunities

11	P8	Establishing specialized centers in schools/clubs/cultural centers and public libraries
12	CL5	Encouraging and supporting NGOs working in this field
13	CL2	Internet based programs is less costly. Schools and students could be encouraged to access such web-sites, which would avail part of this training and exposure- by offering gifts and prizes.
15	E4	Widen the scope of training and exposure opportunities during high school and faculty years
16	Y8	Eliminate/fight any attempt to suppress the creativity in young generation and condescending attitude incompetent adults exert out of their level of authority
17	P6	International exposure, and change in work and volunteering values
18	CL3	Spread information about foreign student exchange programs
19	Y5	Involving civil society more in providing more of such opportunities
20	CL1	Opportunities need to be part of the school curricula
21	Y2	Electronic libraries, community volunteer teaching and training
22	Edu2	Engagement programs where potential leaders are exposed to opportunities to lead and organize under supervision
23	Edu3	Offer students more opportunities even with their local communities to take the lead
24	P4	Networking with national and international development agencies
25	Edu5	Design modules, activities, meetings, workshops, seminars
26	CL4	More Programs for the youth with different aspects

b. Lack of funding and infrastructure required to develop leadership programs

Sequence	Stakeholder	Suggestions
2 develop leadership	CL6	Private schools must support public schools in funding and infrastructure required to develop leadership programs via projects of community service applied in the international schools.
3 implemented by	P7	You can work this through businesses that nurture leadership like a major ones done implemented by
4 for planning	Edu1	ECG, Orascom and other NGOs
		Small gatherings in Mosques outside prayer times for all denominations, and only for planning community development and guidance. The groups will plan what best to do for their community, hence
5	Y3	practice leadership without arrogance and superiority.
6	Edu4	I do not think it needs that much funding it needs organization and dedication
7	E1	Internships
8 other org e.g. AGTBE	P2	At this point, I guess we can only get funds from abroad
		Make deals with large companies like internships, seek volunteers from NGOs or other org e.g. AGTBE
10 funding and learning	P1	Come up with fundraising concerts, charities and bazaars which can help in getting funding and learning more about the issues at hand
11	P8	Private sector support

12	CL5	Governmental and civic society institutions (Ministry of youth, Ministries of
education and higher		education, community service clubs as Rotary) should contribute to the funding of
		such activities.
13	CL2	Part of the funding should be directed towards the recruiting process for potential
leaders, and then the		significant part to be directed towards training the relatively few potential leaders
		(you have to do with
		what you have).
14	P3	Micro-financing
15	E4	Seeking the support of big companies and businessmen to provide internships
16	Y8	Funding is never a problem, there are many local and foreign bodies who are ready
to sponsor brilliant		youth. The challenge will be to fight any corruption existing in the chain of
		command in the program
17	P6	Focus on content and methodology of training and activities, rather than logistics
18	CL3	Seek support and funding from businessmen and companies as part of their corporate
social		responsibility
19	Y5	Trying to develop such programs as part of the educational opportunities offered by
the government		
20	CL1	Well, if it is a priority with our government then there would be no lack of funding
since schools will		

		offer skill building and opportunities.
21	Y2	Donors can help
22	Edu2	Use existing institutions, placements, internships where the candidate provides service in return for training
23	Edu3	Governmental and NGOs can support the funding process
24	P4	Forming community participation programs and mobilizing donors
25	Edu5	Fundraising activities, NGOs, look for cost effective means
26	CL4	Multinational companies should play a very important role in the social contribution

c. Negative family influences, mindset of parents/adults not believing in youth leadership

Sequence	Stakeholder	Suggestions
2	CL6	National and social Associations must provide more trainings and workshops to overcome and change negative family influences, mindset of parents/adults not believing in youth leadership.
3	P4	Paradigm shift can take place through REAL opportunities offered to youth after training and also building FAITH and TRUST in our country as well as training Leaders and managers that Youth will not create the sense of 'My Position is at Risk"
4	Edu1	Only by example and lack of prejudices will the parents accept the new trend. If only one group leads

5	Y3	the good example the rest will follow. Monitors of such programs should be trained to the highest standards.
6	Edu4	This is a mess and no one size fits all in Egypt
7	E1	Awareness for the parents and whole family sessions with experts Psychological help on school should be there
8	P2	Awareness campaigns for parents, seek sponsorship from companies e.g. Vodafone, Coke, Cadbury, Nestle, etc.
9	CL8	Very difficult to change
10	P1	Show parents examples of young great leaders, using the media to dispel such negativity by providing exposure to young local and international leaders
11	P8	Schools and centers talking to parents to make them understand
12	CL5	Awareness programs targeting parents through NGOs working in this field and social media
13	CL2	In every opportunity give parents something to look forward to, e.g. free fellowship at a private university, or in coordination with ministry of higher education, a few guaranteed number of opportunities to join top colleges of their choices (like medicine and engineering) even with a lower GPA than thanaweyya aamma. Give stories of success to be recited in schools, websites, or every media

possible, so that parents hope they can be proud of their children the same way parents of previously

chosen future leaders are.

14	P3	School activities
15	E4	Focusing on negative practices and educate youth on how to manage them
16	Y8	Awarding potential leaders is key! If the young adult is properly recognized for their

own efforts, they

will gain the strong will to fight for their thoughts even with the presence of negative influence. But

once they lose hope in the social structure banning their growth, no motivation will

ever work!

17	P6	Awareness for the elders through media and parents workshops with psychologists
18	CL3	Dialogue and compromise
19	Y5	Provide mentorship and advisory boards in schools and through leadership programs

to provide young

leaders with self esteem needed for developing their leadership skills and self belief

| 20 | CL1 | This is a generation issue that has always existed. If schools and NGOs give |

leadership opportunities,

more and more parents will be changing their minds.

| 22 | Edu2 | Work harder on environment |
| 23 | Edu3 | Workshop and TV Shows and programs focusing on youth leadership and |

encouraging parents to give

youth the opportunity to lead

24	P4 development	Establishing publications and dialogue groups with advocates of leadership
25	Edu5	Orientations and awareness raising meetings, show examples and success stories
26	CL4	This will take time but can be done through showing a lot of youth role models

d. Lack of skilled and knowledgeable trainers/coaches/counselors to discover leadership talents, offer support and

mentoring, and provide feedback and guidance

Sequence	Stakeholder	Suggestions
2	CL6 good way	Provide more internal and external trainings and workshops in order to prepare in a
		trainers/coaches/counselors to easily discover leadership talents, offer support and mentoring, and
		provide feedback and guidance.
3 as introducing	P7	Certifying trainers and also highlighting the work of trainers in organization as well
		Career Paths programs in companies
4 and trainers will only	Edu1	It does not come overnight. A period of enunciation is necessary. Skilled coaches
		come up after a period of enlightenment and proper training. To have the first leaders, a lot has to be invested, money, time and support. Sponsorships by different organizations could be a good starting point as long as the choice of the candidate is not based on favoritism.

5	Y3	This is a long term thing that needs a lot of planning
6	Edu4	Training and mentoring to get new generation of them
7	E1	NGOs should take part in that
8	P2	They are there but seek high charges. Seek volunteers who would have eldership practical experience rather than academic experience. Try to make an atmosphere of exchange like mother and daughter day at work or father and son, or family summer training. Would be great if a mom or dad is able to take youth to work in holidays and expose them to small tasks like copying, filing, etc. They will observe managers and capture leadership by example
9	CL8	More trainers and more model leaders
10	P1	Every school should develop a counseling/mentoring program made up of trained and qualified individuals who are able to spot the talented individuals. To draw student's attention to the importance of feedback and proper guidance.
11	P8	Training of trainers and exchange programs
12	CL5	Tailored programs for preparing adults to work in this field. Academic programs for professionals and simplified ones through specialized NGOs for volunteers.
13	CL2	The same way as (a) above, designing web sites with full programs is relatively cheaper and could be

widespread through offering prizes and gifts. The possibility of a promotion -in coordination with ministry of education- for those who pass the web site program or exam or competition would give a definite edge.

| 15 | E4 | Development plans for teachers and academics to be able to play such a role |
| 16 | Y8 | This is a long-term plan: 1. You need to prepare a qualified caliber to pass on the information |

adequately (it doesn't need to be in large group). 2. By selecting potential candidate you build a second line of trainers who are ready to support but lack the opportunity. 3. Final level is to outreach to the real young leaders. This might open the door to the coming generation to become better and the current generation need to accept the mission to sacrifice their own benefit for a better future to our country

17	P6	Online mentoring, local experts volunteering, enhancing the habit of helping others
18	CL3	Look for and train potential trainers and create a national database for skilled coaches and trainers
20	CL1	Leaders in an field should be certified and skilled. This in itself will allow them to be mindful of

potential leaders. In Egypt, we lack specialized teachers, trainers, coaches and counselors.

21	Y2	Training the trainer program
22	Edu2	Train the training (TOT) programs, search committees
23	Edu3	TOT programs for brilliant students to become wonderful coaches and trainers

24	P4	Train social and psychological specialists in education system
25	Edu5	Design a trainer of trainers program and build on that followed by a chain of trainings
26	CL4	I think we should take care of them first to have a good structure and base for teaching a very powerful generation of youth

Appendix K: Thank You Message for Completing the Three Questionnaires

Thank You Message for Completing the Three Questionnaires

Thank you for taking the time to participate in my research study. I appreciate taking the time to complete the three rounds of questionnaires. Without your support and all of the other participants, this study would not be possible. If you have any questions or concerns, please feel free to contact me at xxxxxxxxxxxx@email.phoenix.edu or xxx-xxx-xxxx.

Thank you!

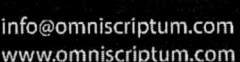 

Printed by
Schaltungsdienst Lange o.H.G., Berlin